JD Vance

The Hillbilly Outsider Who Became America's Vice President

Preston D. Munro

ISBN: 9798310940475

Every effort was made to produce a factually accurate book. However, the author and publisher are not liable for any errors, oversights, or omissions.

Table of Contents

Preston D. Munro

"The American Dream is not that every man must be level with every other man. The American Dream is that every man must be free to become whatever God intends he should become." — Ronald Reagan

Prologue: The Oath of Office

On January 20, 2025, the Capitol Building buzzed with the anticipation of history being made. Under blue skies that belied the chill in the air, Washington, D.C. anxiously awaited the moment when history would be made: the inauguration of Donald Trump for a second term as U.S. president. By Trump's side? The man whose meteoric rise played a key role in securing a landslide victory in the November 2024 election: JD Vance. The man who was about to become America's fiftieth vice president, ushering in a new era for the nation.

Outside, it was a bright winter day—sunny, but cold and blustery. A deep freeze had settled in, and sharp gusts of wind cut through the city's landmarks, chilling those outside to the bone. The cloudless sky stretched in a brilliant, brittle blue, its brightness stark against the bone-chilling cold. Historically, presidential inaugurations are held outdoors, but the uncharacteristic chill—27°F at noon, with a wind chill temperature of 14°F—had forced a rare shift. And so, the ceremony was moved inside, where the warmth of the ornate

Rotunda, normally a space reserved for somber reflection and moments of national significance, provided an appropriate backdrop for this monumental occasion.

With its soaring dome and iconic frescoed ceiling, the Rotunda provided a strikingly intimate setting for what is typically a grand outdoor spectacle. Rows of chairs stretched beneath statues of America's most revered figures, creating a stage that felt both timeless and deeply personal. The atmosphere was warm, reverent, and infused with a sense of history. Flickering chandeliers cast golden light over the faces of the gathered attendees, heightening the ceremony's intimacy. The enclosed space allowed every word and gesture to resonate with immediacy, matching the gravity of the occasion. The echoes of quiet conversations by attendees—among them, America's tech elite and billionaire set—reverberated softly against the marble walls. The sound of footsteps blended into the hum of cameras and microphones that broadcast the ceremony to millions watching from afar all over the world.

Though smaller than the expansive crowd that would have filled the National Mall, the audience exuded a palpable energy. This was a moment to remember: JD Vance, whose story had captivated the nation, would take the oath of office as Vice President of the United States. The symbolism of his journey from poverty in Middletown, Ohio, to the Capitol's inner sanctum exemplified the American Dream at its very best.

The limited seating capacity in the Rotunda meant that only the most prominent figures in American politics and society were present. Former presidents sat shoulder to shoulder in the front rows, their expressions reflecting the gravity of the moment. Across the aisle, members of Congress, Supreme Court justices, and Cabinet members filled the remaining seats. Their presence captured the bipartisan significance of the event, a nod to the continuity of American democracy even in divisive times.

President Donald Trump, seated near the podium, commanded attention as he exchanged brief nods and handshakes with attendees. His endorsement of JD Vance had been a pivotal moment in their shared political journey, and today marked the culmination of that alliance. International ambassadors, cultural icons, and leaders of industry watched with rapt attention, gathered to witness history unfold.

Amid the dignitaries and officials, JD Vance's wife, Usha Vance, exuded quiet grace. Dressed in a peony pink cashmere coat from Oscar de la Renta, she smiled faintly, her composure a testament to her role as a steadying force throughout JD's rise in prominence.

When JD Vance approached the podium, the room fell into a hushed silence. His three young children were escorted in to watch the proceedings. Supreme Court Justice Brett Kavanaugh stood ready. At Vance's left, Usha held their toddler daughter in her arms, while his two sons looked on, dressed just like Dad in navy suits. The Vance children's gaze darted between the majestic surroundings and their father. For them, this day was both extraordinary and deeply familiar—a culmination of the countless hours their family had spent traveling, campaigning, and supporting JD's ambitions.

Vance's gaze was steady, his face set with determination and humility as he raised his right hand. His voice, steady and resonant, filled the Rotunda as he repeated the phrases, each syllable enunciated with precision and clarity. The gravity of the occasion was evident not only in his tone but in the deliberate pace of his delivery, as though each word was a promise he intended to keep.

The words would seal his place in history and elevate him to the position of vice president of the United States: "I, James David Vance, do solemnly swear that I will support and defend the Constitution of the United States against all enemies, foreign and domestic. That I will bear true faith and allegiance to the same. That I take this obligation freely without any mental reservations or purpose of evasion. And that I will well and faithfully discharge the duties of the office of which I am about to enter. So help me God."[1]

As he finished the oath, his lips curled into a faint, almost imperceptible smile—a rare moment of emotion breaking through his otherwise composed exterior. The Supreme Court Justice congratulated him and the applause filled the Rotunda, a crescendo of appreciation and anticipation. For JD Vance, this was the culmination of a political journey and a deeply symbolic moment. Here, within the hallowed walls of the Capitol, he stood as proof of the enduring promise of America: that even a boy from Middletown, a self-proclaimed Appalachian hillbilly shaped by poverty and hardship, could rise to the second-highest office in the land.

And it was only the beginning.

---

[1] "Video shows JD Vance take oath as 50th vice president on Inauguration Day," USA Today.

"It is not in the stars to hold our destiny but in ourselves."
— William Shakespeare

Introduction

Next door to the White House lies one of the most architecturally striking and historically significant buildings in all of Washington, D.C. Known as the Eisenhower Executive Office Building, or EEOB, it was constructed between 1871 and 1888 in French-inspired Second Empire Style, with an ornate façade. Inside, key decision-makers of the U.S. government carry out their daily work in offices including the National Security Council, the Office of Management and Budget, and the Vice President's Ceremonial Office.

The Vice President's Ceremonial Office is a study in contrasts. Beneath the grand chandeliers and gilded moldings, the room hums with the quiet efficiency of a modern political machine. And at the heart of it all is JD Vance—a man whose early years were shaped by instability, addiction, and poverty. Yet despite this unlikely background, Vance now occupies one of the most powerful offices in the nation.

From the outside, Vance presents the polished image of a national leader. His tailored navy suits, impeccable posture, measured tone, and steady demeanor speak to the refinement earned through years of navigating elite institutions like Yale Law School and the U.S.

Senate. But beneath the bright blue eyes and polished exterior lies a core forged in the blue-collar world of Middletown, Ohio, a struggling Rust Belt town where resilience was necessary to survive. This duality is what makes Vance so compelling: he is both a product of his past and a master of his present.

The story of JD Vance is, at its heart, an American story, one that illustrates the enduring possibility of the American Dream while grappling with the barriers that often obstruct it. Born into a family defined by chaos and hardship, Vance's early life was shaped by his mother's battle with addiction, the instability of multiple father figures coming in and out of his life, and the oppressive economic despair of a town left behind by industrial decline. Yet, even in those years, there were glimmers of the man he would become—a boy who found solace in the fierce love of his grandparents, Mamaw and Papaw, and who dared to dream of something more.

Today, Vance embodies the tension between two worlds: the grit of his working-class roots and the polish of the corridors of power. As vice president, he serves as a bridge between those who feel forgotten by Washington and the institutions tasked with shaping the nation's future. His epic journey from Middletown to the White House offers us a lens through which to view the struggles and aspirations of millions of Americans.

Vance's path to the vice presidency is nothing short of dramatic. From enlisting in the Marines to escape the chaos of his youth, to navigating the culture shock of Yale Law School, to the national acclaim that followed the publication of his memoir *Hillbilly Elegy*, his story reads like the script of a Hollywood drama. But unlike a neatly packaged narrative, Vance's journey is peppered with contradictions and complexities. His transition from author to politician—and, indeed, from an early and outspoken critic of Donald Trump to his loyal running mate and second-in-command of the free world—reveals a man constantly evolving, recalibrating his identity to meet the demands of his ambitions.

To understand what makes JD Vance tick, we must examine the chapters of his life, exploring the forces that shaped him, the values that drive him, and the controversies that have followed him. From the bleak streets of Middletown, Ohio, to the marbled halls of Washington, Vance's story exemplifies resilience and reinvention, ambition and authenticity. It is the story of a man who has become a symbol of both the promise and the challenges of modern America.

Vance's nontraditional, non-linear journey is what shaped him into the leader he has become. His childhood instability and hardship taught him the importance of resilience and the value of strong family bonds. The discipline instilled in him by the Marines prepared him for the rigors of public life, while his time at Yale sharpened his intellect and gave him the tools to navigate elite institutions. Publishing his candid memoir not only brought him fame but also positioned him as a voice for America's forgotten communities.

Looking back at his trajectory, we can see how each experience built upon the last, culminating in Vance's decision to enter politics. As a senator and now vice president, Vance draws on these myriad experiences to craft policies and advocate for those who feel left behind. The challenges of his youth inform his empathy and approach to reshaping America in a new vision, while the lessons learned along the way shape his leadership style.

While Vance's rise is remarkable, his current place as vice president presents a new set of challenges. On the national stage, the stakes are higher, the scrutiny more intense, and the obstacles more daunting. As the vice president of the United States, he must navigate the complexities of governance, work to bridge divides within a polarized nation, and prove that his populist message can translate into meaningful change. His tenure as vice president is the ultimate test of the ideals he has championed throughout his life.

Ultimately, Vance's life to date reflects the struggles, aspirations, and hopes of modern America. His rise from a troubled boy in small-town Ohio to a leader representing the world's greatest nation on the international stage embodies the promise and complexity of the American Dream. It shows us all that with resilience, ambition, and daring to strive for our true potential, we each have the power to transform our lives—and our world—at any stage.

As we look back on the experiences that brought JD Vance to the White House, we do so with the understanding that his journey is emblematic of something larger. It is a testament to the strength of the human spirit, the possibilities of opportunity, and the challenges of leadership in a divided nation. The chapters ahead explore these themes in depth, shedding light on how one man's story intersects with the broader narrative of America in the twenty-first century.

The stage is set, the spotlight is bright, and Vice President JD Vance stands ready. This is his story—and the story of the nation he has been elected to serve.

"The test of our progress is not whether we add more to the abundance of those who have much; it is whether we provide enough for those who have too little."
— Franklin D. Roosevelt

Middletown, Ohio: A Town on the Brink

Middletown was once the epitome of the American Dream for blue-collar families. Located between Dayton and Cincinnati in southwest Ohio, the town was built around the sprawling steel mills of Armco (later AK Steel). Middletown thrived in the mid-twentieth century as a hub of industrial production that offered stable jobs, good wages, and a path to the middle class for countless families who migrated from places like Appalachia in search of opportunity. The Vance family was one of them, pulled by the allure of possibility.

But by the time JD Vance was born in 1984, Middletown's glory days were long behind it. The mills that had powered the town's prosperity were laying off workers, victims of globalization, automation, and declining demand. Unemployment rose steadily, casting a shadow over the community. Once-proud neighborhoods began to show signs of decay—empty storefronts, abandoned houses, and streets quieter than they had been in decades. The optimism that had defined Middletown was giving way to despair.

Despite the town's economic struggles, Middletown clung fiercely to its cultural values: hard work, family loyalty, and resilience in the face of adversity. These principles were passed down through generations, forming the bedrock of the community's identity. Yet, the economic downturn tested these values in profound ways. The loss of steady jobs hurt families financially, and worse, it eroded their sense of purpose and pride. Addiction, particularly to prescription opioids, began to take hold, compounding the challenges faced by families like Vance's.

Speaking at a rally in his hometown during the 2024 election campaign, Vance reflected, "My life wasn't all that different from a lot of people who grew up in Middletown, Ohio. It was tough, but it was surrounded by loving people, and it was surrounded by something that if we don't fight for is not going to be around for the next generation of kids, and that's opportunity."[2]

For Vance, Middletown was both home and a source of frustration. He loved the sense of community and the stories of grit that defined his town, but he also saw the ways in which economic hardship and cultural stagnation held people back.

*   *   *

Jackson, Kentucky, in the heart of Appalachia, was where Vance's family story began. Nestled in the hills of Breathitt County, Jackson was a small town shaped by the coal industry, close-knit communities, and a deep connection to the land. Life there was tough but straightforward, governed by traditions that had been passed down for generations. It was a place where family ties were paramount,

---

[2] Stephen Fowler, "JD Vance Vows to Fight for 'forgotten Communities' in Hometown Rally," NPR, July 22, 2024, https://www.npr.org/2024/07/22/nx-s1-5048679/jd-vance-middletown-ohio-rally-kamala-harris-joe-biden.

neighbors looked out for one another, and pride in one's roots ran deep.

Vance's grandparents, Bonnie and James Vance, were products of this Appalachian culture. Known by Vance as "Mamaw" and "Papaw," they, like many families in the region, eventually migrated to Ohio in search of better opportunities. This migration was part of a broader wave of Appalachian diaspora during the mid-twentieth century, as coal jobs dried up and industrial towns in the Midwest promised a new start. For the Vances, that promise was in Middletown, where Papaw found work in the steel mills.

Though they left Jackson behind physically, Mamaw and Papaw carried their Appalachian identity with them to Ohio when they moved after World War II. This culture shaped Vance's upbringing in countless ways. The toughness and fierce independence of Mamaw, the pride Papaw took in his work, and the storytelling that defined family gatherings all had their roots in the Appalachian tradition. Even in Middletown, reminders of Jackson were never far away—photos of the Kentucky hills, Mamaw's insistence on certain values, and summer visits back to the region kept the connection alive.

Appalachian culture also brought its struggles. The pride and loyalty that defined the region could sometimes make it difficult to adapt to change. A reluctance to seek help or admit vulnerability was deeply ingrained, and this cultural trait often exacerbated issues like addiction and economic hardship. For Vance, these complexities were part of his family's story, influencing how he understood both himself and the world around him.

In *Hillbilly Elegy*, Vance describes Mamaw as a "violent nondrunk"[3] and Papaw as a "nonviolent drunk," hinting at the dysfunctional dynamics that marked his family upbringing. The stories he tells support this idea, illustrating the struggles that he and many with similar backgrounds faced.

The story of Middletown and Jackson is, in many ways, the story of working-class America—communities built on hard work and hope, now grappling with the challenges of economic transformation and cultural identity. For Vance, these two towns were symbols of the forces that shaped his early life. Middletown represented the promise of opportunity and the reality of its decline. Jackson embodied the strength and struggles of Appalachian culture, the roots that tethered his family even as they sought a better future.

These places—and the values, challenges, and traditions they carried—formed the foundation of JD's identity. They taught him resilience, shaped his understanding of community, and gave him a unique perspective on the challenges facing rural and blue-collar America.

At the heart of JD Vance's early life was a family torn between love and chaos, stability and dysfunction. Poverty and addiction cast long shadows over his childhood, creating an environment where moments of tenderness were often overshadowed by instability and fear. Vance's personal struggles mirrored a larger crisis gripping working-class America, where families like his were caught in cycles of despair fueled by economic decline and the opioid epidemic.

---

[3] J. D. Vance, *Hillbilly Elegy*, 2016.

Vance later compared it to being akin to learned helplessness, believing his choices had no effect on the way his life would unfold.

Vance's childhood was marred by instability that went beyond the typical challenges of growing up. His family often moved house, driven by financial difficulties and the instability of his mother's relationships. Sometimes, they would relocate within Middletown; other times, they would find themselves in entirely new neighborhoods. Each move disrupted Vance's sense of security, leaving him feeling untethered and uncertain about what lay ahead.

The financial struggles were unrelenting. Bills piled up, and money was always tight, creating an atmosphere of stress that permeated their home. These hardships were daily realities that shaped how Vance understood the world. He learned early on that survival meant improvising, enduring, and finding solace in small moments of stability when they came.

The chaos of Vance's upbringing centered around his mother, Bev, whose struggle with addiction defined much of his childhood. Bev was a nurse, but her battle with substance abuse undermined her ability to provide the stability her children needed. Prescription drugs became her escape from the pressures of life, pulling her deeper into a cycle of dependence and emotional volatility.

Bev's addiction strained her relationships, leading to a string of failed marriages and transient partners who entered and exited Vance's life. For a young boy, these revolving relationships created an unsettling dynamic—just as he began to grow accustomed to one father figure, another would take his place. The lack of continuity left Vance yearning for a sense of permanence that never seemed to come.

The impact of Bev's addiction extended beyond the household. Her frequent absences, erratic behavior, and outbursts of anger created an environment of uncertainty. Vance endured arguments that escalated into violence, nights spent wondering if his mother would come home, and the emotional toll of seeing someone he loved succumb to addiction.

Growing up in such a turbulent environment took an emotional toll on Vance. He often felt like he was walking on eggshells, never knowing when the next crisis would strike. The unpredictability of his mother's behavior forced him to mature quickly, taking on responsibilities far beyond his years. At times, he had to shield himself emotionally, retreating into books or school as a way to escape the chaos at home.

Instances of neglect added to his challenges. Meals were missed, routines were disrupted, and basic needs were sometimes overlooked. Yet, despite the hardships, Vance also experienced moments of deep love and care, particularly from his grandparents, Mamaw and Papaw, who served as his anchors during times of upheaval. Their influence gave him glimpses of what stability could look like, even as his immediate household spiraled out of control.

Some of the most formative moments of Vance's childhood were born from fear—fear of losing his mother to addiction, fear of the violence that sometimes erupted in their home, and fear of a future that seemed increasingly uncertain. These experiences shaped his early worldview, instilling in him both a deep-seated anxiety and an incredible capacity for resilience.

While the instability could have broken him, Vance found ways to cope and adapt. He sought refuge in school, where teachers often recognized his potential, and in the unwavering support of his grandparents, who believed in his ability to rise above his circumstances. These glimpses of hope became lifelines, helping him endure and ultimately inspiring him to strive for a better future.

Vance's family struggles were not unique—they were echoes of a larger crisis unfolding in working-class America. The challenges were rooted in systemic issues that affected entire communities. The loss of stable, well-paying jobs in towns like Middletown eroded the social fabric, leaving families vulnerable to crises they were ill-equipped to handle. Addiction, once seen as a personal failing, was increasingly understood as a symptom of deeper societal problems: a lack of opportunity, inadequate healthcare, and a fraying sense of hope. The economic decline created fertile ground for despair, and the opioid epidemic swept through these communities with devastating consequences. Families like Vance's were left to navigate the wreckage, caught in a web of addiction, unemployment, and broken systems that offered little support.

Bev's battle with addiction mirrored the experiences of countless others. What had once been a means of relief—prescription painkillers meant to dull physical and emotional pain—quickly spiraled into dependence. The epidemic, fueled by overprescription and corporate greed, took lives, tore families apart, and left children like Vance to pick up the pieces.

Vance's childhood was defined by the twin forces of love and chaos. His mother's struggles with addiction and the instability of his home life could have derailed his future. Yet, through resilience and the support of his grandparents, he found a way to navigate the turmoil and emerge stronger.

Mamaw and Papaw were the constants he could rely on—two larger-than-life figures who, in their own unique ways, provided the stability and love that kept him grounded. They were not perfect, far from it, but their influence shaped Vance's sense of identity, resilience, and hope for a better future. Together, they became his refuge, offering him a fighting chance to rise above his circumstances.

Mamaw, or Bonnie Vance, was not the kind of grandmother who baked cookies or coddled her grandchildren. She was a force of nature—sharp-tongued, fiercely independent, and utterly unyielding in her love for Vance. Her colorful personality was matched by her even more colorful language, which she wielded with precision, whether to offer tough love or to make a point so sharp it left no room for debate.

Mamaw's fierce devotion to Vance often manifested in unconventional ways. She wasn't afraid to lay down the law, whether it meant demanding that he take his schoolwork seriously or ensuring he avoided the pitfalls she saw consuming others in their community. For Vance, her no-nonsense approach was both intimidating and inspiring—a constant reminder that she believed in him even when he struggled to believe in himself.

Mamaw's parenting style was as unorthodox as her personality. Once, when Vance confessed that he had cheated on a test, Mamaw didn't scold him in the traditional sense. Instead, she launched into a tirade about integrity, peppered with choice words that made it clear cheating was unacceptable, not because it was against the rules, but because it was beneath him. Her lessons often came wrapped in wit and humor, but their impact was profound.

One of the most vivid memories Vance recounted involved Mamaw's sheer determination to protect him. After an altercation between Vance and his mother turned violent, Mamaw took him in, making it clear to everyone involved that her grandson's safety was non-negotiable.

Amidst the chaos of his home life, Mamaw's house became a sanctuary for Vance. It wasn't always calm—Mamaw's temper could be as fiery as her love—but it was a place where he felt safe and supported. She made sure he had a quiet space to study, a roof over his head, and the encouragement to dream bigger than his circumstances. Mamaw's influence was transformative, giving Vance the foundation he needed to envision a future beyond Middletown's struggles.

In contrast to Mamaw's fiery personality, Papaw, or James Vance, was a quieter presence in Vance's life. A former coal miner turned steelworker, he embodied the working-class values of hard work, humility, and loyalty. While Mamaw was the loud protector, Papaw provided a steadying influence, teaching Vance the importance of responsibility and perseverance.

Papaw didn't speak in grand proclamations, but his actions left a lasting impression on Vance. He showed up for work every day, took pride in providing for his family, and found solace in the simple pleasures of life, like sitting in his recliner with a glass of Mountain Dew. His calm demeanor balanced Mamaw's intensity, creating a dynamic that gave Vance a unique perspective on resilience and partnership.

Papaw was not without his flaws. For much of Vance's early life, he battled alcoholism, a struggle that caused friction within the family and often tested his relationships. Vance remembers Papaw as both a source of stability and, at times, a cause of instability. Yet, in his later years, Papaw made a conscious effort to reform. He stopped drinking and began to repair the damage caused by his addiction, showing Vance that redemption was possible even in the face of deep personal struggles.

Papaw's journey left a lasting impression on Vance. It taught him that change was not only possible but necessary, and it gave him a firsthand understanding of the complexities of addiction. Papaw's ability to confront his demons became a powerful example for Vance, shaping how he viewed responsibility, accountability, and growth.

Mamaw and Papaw's relationship was far from perfect. Their arguments were legendary—often loud, occasionally explosive—but beneath the bickering was a deep, unshakable bond. They balanced each other in ways that, while unconventional, worked for them. Papaw's quiet steadiness tempered Mamaw's fiery outbursts, while her fierce determination pushed him to confront issues he might otherwise have ignored.

Vance grew up watching their dynamic, learning lessons about love, resilience, and teamwork along the way. Their shared goal of raising Vance to rise above his circumstances united them, even when their personalities clashed. They were a team, bound by their love for their grandson and their hope that he could escape the cycles of poverty and addiction that had shaped their own lives.

Together, Mamaw and Papaw created an environment where Vance could thrive despite the chaos surrounding him. They made sacrifices to ensure he had opportunities they never did, from encouraging his education to providing him with a stable home when his mother couldn't. Their influence gave Vance the tools he needed to navigate the challenges of his childhood and envision a future beyond Middletown.

*   *   *

Poverty wasn't just an abstract concept for JD Vance—it was a daily reality, woven into the fabric of his childhood. It was the constant undercurrent of his family's struggles, shaping their lives in ways that were both visible and hidden. Coupled with the shadow of addiction, poverty created a landscape of instability, fear, and frustration that permeated not just Vance's home but the entire community of Middletown. Yet even in the darkest moments, there were glimmers of hope—small but significant reminders that better days might still lie ahead.

The challenges of growing up in a low-income household were ever-present. Food insecurity was a frequent concern. Dinner often meant making do with what little was in the fridge, and meals were stretched to last longer than they should. Vance recalls moments when his family would rely on processed, calorie-heavy foods simply because they were affordable, even as the health consequences of such diets loomed. Financial stress hung over every decision—whether it was deciding which bills to pay, struggling to afford basic school supplies, or facing the constant threat of eviction.

Healthcare was another persistent issue. Trips to the doctor were rare and usually only occurred in emergencies. Preventative care or dental visits were luxuries Vance's family couldn't afford, and untreated ailments became a part of life. Vance learned early on that survival often meant enduring discomfort and making sacrifices.

Addiction compounded these struggles, casting a long shadow. His mother's dependence on prescription painkillers and later other substances brought chaos into their home. Worst of all, addiction was a public burden, one that carried an unshakable stigma. Vance remembers the sideways glances and hushed conversations from neighbors and teachers, the unspoken judgment that came with being part of a family marked by addiction.

The isolation that accompanied this stigma was palpable. Vance often felt like an outsider, even within his own community. He carried the weight of his family's reputation, knowing that his mother's struggles weren't just hers—they reflected on him as well. This sense of shame and invisibility became an additional hurdle, making it even harder to imagine a way out.

The challenges the Vance family faced were mirrored across Middletown. As the town's industrial base crumbled, the community infrastructure that once supported families began to erode. Schools, once a source of stability, struggled to adapt to the growing number of students dealing with trauma and poverty. Teachers were overworked, resources were stretched thin, and extracurricular programs that could have offered a reprieve for children like Vance were cut back or eliminated entirely.

Community resources, such as social services and public health programs, also suffered under the weight of economic decline. Libraries, recreation centers, and other communal spaces either closed their doors or became underfunded shadows of what they once were. For many families, these losses compounded the challenges of daily life, leaving them with fewer places to turn for support.

Vance was not alone in his struggles. Many of his peers and neighbors faced similar challenges, and their experiences helped him understand the larger dynamics of poverty and addiction. He saw classmates who came to school hungry, their concentration dulled by empty stomachs. He noticed friends who dropped out, unable to balance the demands of school with the pressures of chaotic home lives or the need to contribute financially to their families.

The opioid crisis, which would later dominate headlines, was already beginning to take hold. Vance observed its devastating impact on his neighbors and friends, watching as promising futures were cut short by addiction. These experiences planted seeds of understanding in Vance, helping him recognize that his family's struggles were part of a broader systemic issue, extending far beyond the walls of his home.

Amid the difficulties, Vance found moments of hope—small, fleeting instances that reminded him that life could be different. Teachers played a crucial role in these moments. Some went out of their way to encourage Vance, recognizing his potential even when he struggled to see it himself. A kind word, extra attention, or praise for a well-written essay became lifelines, offering him a sense of validation and possibility.

Neighbors, too, occasionally stepped in to fill gaps left by his family's struggles. A neighbor might offer a warm meal, a place to stay during a particularly volatile night, or simply a kind gesture that made Vance feel seen and cared for. These acts of kindness, while not erasing the hardships, gave him the strength to keep going.

School became one of the few places where Vance could find a sense of control and accomplishment. A good grade on a test, recognition for a project, or praise from a teacher provided moments of pride that counterbalanced the chaos at home. These small victories were symbolic of the life he hoped to build, one where hard work and perseverance could lead to a brighter future.

For Vance, the scars left by poverty and addiction would take years to heal. Yet these same experiences also forged a deep well of resilience and empathy, qualities that would define him as a leader. The daily struggles of low-income life, the stigma of addiction, and the broader decline of Middletown taught Vance hard lessons about survival and endurance. But the moments of hope—small gestures, kind words, and glimpses of possibility—provided him with the fuel to dream of something better.

*   *   *

Even amidst the chaos of his early life, Vance exhibited signs of a natural curiosity and quiet determination that set him apart from many of his peers. While his childhood was defined by poverty and instability, it was also marked by a growing awareness that he could carve out a different future for himself. Through his innate intelligence, early academic achievements, and moments of guidance from mentors, Vance began to show the first signs of the ambition that would later propel him to national prominence.

Vance's thirst for knowledge became apparent at a young age. Books were his first window into a world beyond Middletown, a way to imagine lives and places far removed from his own. From the school library to well-worn novels borrowed from friends, reading gave him a sense of escape and possibility. Through stories, he encountered characters who faced adversity and triumphed, reinforcing his budding belief that change was possible.

He devoured anything he could get his hands on, from biographies of historical figures to science fiction novels that sparked his imagination. One teacher recalled Vance's habit of staying after class to talk about the themes of a book or the meaning behind a particular passage, always probing deeper than most kids his age. His questions revealed a mind that wasn't content with surface-level understanding—he wanted to know why things were the way they were and how they could be different.

Vance's natural curiosity extended beyond books. He often asked thoughtful, sometimes challenging, questions about the world around him. Why did some people seem to thrive while others struggled? Why were the factories closing, and what did that mean for families like his? These were the kinds of questions that many adults in his community avoided or dismissed, but Vance couldn't ignore them.

This critical thinking set him apart early on. While others might have accepted their circumstances as unchangeable, Vance wanted to understand the root causes. That curiosity became the foundation for his later ability to analyze complex social and economic issues, a skill that would serve him well in his career as a writer and policymaker.

In the classroom, Vance's potential began to emerge, even as his home life remained tumultuous. Though there were times when the chaos at home affected his focus, he demonstrated a natural aptitude for learning that caught the attention of his teachers. Math, reading, and history became areas where he excelled, often earning praise that gave him a sense of accomplishment in an otherwise uncertain world.

Teachers played a crucial role in nurturing Vance's abilities. One middle school teacher, in particular, recognized his potential and encouraged him to think beyond the limitations of his immediate environment. She saw not just a student with good grades but a young boy who had the capacity to rise above his circumstances. Vance often credits these small moments of recognition as pivotal in his development, giving him the confidence to believe he was capable of more.

Throughout his early education, a handful of mentors provided critical support. Whether it was a teacher who stayed after class to help him with assignments, a librarian who recommended books tailored to his interests, or a coach who pushed him to apply himself in ways he hadn't considered, these figures reinforced the idea that he was capable of achieving great things.

Mamaw's relentless insistence on the importance of education acted as an additional driving force. She wasn't afraid to hold Vance accountable, often demanding that he focus on his studies and reminding him of the opportunities that education could unlock. Her tough love, coupled with the encouragement of educators who believed in him, created an environment where Vance's academic potential could flourish.

While many of his peers succumbed to the challenges of their environment—dropping out of school, turning to drugs, or settling for low-paying jobs—Vance showed a determination to forge a different path. One moment that stood out was his decision to buckle down and improve his grades during a particularly difficult year. Encouraged by Mamaw and a supportive teacher, he began setting small, achievable goals, like finishing homework on time or studying for tests more diligently. Each success, no matter how small, reinforced his belief that he could rise above his circumstances.

Another time, Mamaw reminded him that the choices he made now would determine the kind of life he would have later. While her words were harsh, they struck a chord with Vance, igniting a sense of urgency to prove her right.

JD's decision to stay focused on his education was not an easy one, especially in a community where many young people saw little value in schooling. But he remained committed, often motivated by a deep desire to escape the cycles of poverty and addiction that had defined his family's life. He set his sights on higher education, even when it felt like an impossible dream.

This drive to succeed was evident in small but telling choices: staying late to work on a project, seeking out mentors for advice, or simply refusing to give up when the odds were stacked against him. Each of these moments added up, paving the way for his eventual success.

While challenges could have easily derailed Vance's future, it was within this crucible of hardship that JD began to develop the traits that would define his life: resilience, grit, and the steadfast belief that a better future was possible. Combined with the values instilled in him by his grandparents and the spark of ambition ignited by his circumstances, Vance's formative years laid the groundwork for his remarkable journey.

These early years were the source of many lessons that would inform Vance's life in the future. Growing up in poverty and witnessing the devastating impact of addiction shaped his worldview profoundly. He saw firsthand how economic instability and social decay could strip people of their dignity and hope. These experiences instilled in Vance a deep sense of empathy—an understanding of what it means to feel trapped by circumstances beyond one's control.

Vance's childhood was a daily lesson in the complexities of human behavior. He learned to see his mother's addiction not simply as a personal failing but as part of a broader crisis affecting countless families like his own. This nuanced perspective would later inform his work as an author and politician, allowing him to speak authentically about the struggles of working-class Americans.

Amid the challenges, Vance developed a remarkable resilience. Every setback—whether it was a financial crisis, a broken promise, or an episode of family turmoil—taught him how to adapt and persevere. The chaos of his home life forced him to grow up quickly, taking on responsibilities that most children his age never had to face.

But rather than succumbing to bitterness or despair, Vance channeled his energy into finding ways to move forward. Whether it was excelling in school, seeking out mentors, or leaning on the tough love of Mamaw and Papaw, Vance demonstrated a level of grit that would become one of his defining characteristics.

Mamaw and Papaw were responsible for instilling his belief in hard work. Serving as his lifeline, they lived by the values of hard work, loyalty, and toughness, and these same values became the foundation upon which Vance built his future. Mamaw's no-nonsense approach to life, paired with Papaw's quiet resilience, taught him that success wasn't handed to anyone—it had to be earned through determination and effort.

Mamaw often reminded Vance that his circumstances didn't have to define him, but it was up to him to take control of his future. Her tough love was always underpinned by a fierce belief in his potential. Papaw, on the other hand, demonstrated perseverance, especially in his efforts to reform his own life after years of struggling with alcoholism.

Together, they created a set of guiding principles that would carry Vance through life: work hard, stay loyal to those who matter, and never give up, no matter how steep the climb.

Ultimately, the hardships Vance faced were motivators. Watching his family struggle and seeing peers succumb to the same cycles of poverty and addiction instilled in him a drive to break free. He didn't want to follow the same path; he wanted to carve out a different future, one that was defined by opportunity rather than limitation.

As a result, Vance's early ambition was about proving that change was possible. He wanted to show that someone from Middletown, Ohio, with all its struggles, could rise to achieve something extraordinary.

Even as a child, Vance's ambition went beyond simply escaping his circumstances. He dreamed of creating a life where he could give back to the community and advocate for those who had been left behind. These early aspirations foreshadowed the man he would become—a leader who sought to bridge the gap between working-class America and the institutions of power.

Whether it was excelling in school, joining the Marines, or later pursuing higher education, Vance's actions were always guided by a vision of something greater. He understood that his success wasn't just about him; it was about the possibility of inspiring others to believe in their own potential.

The lessons Vance learned from hardship, the values instilled by his grandparents, and the spark of ambition ignited by his early experiences all came together to form the foundation of his future. His ability to navigate challenges with resilience, his commitment to hard work, and his desire to make a difference became the cornerstones of his identity.

These formative years remain central to understanding Vance's journey to the White House. They are a testament to the power of grit, the influence of family, and the belief that even in the face of overwhelming adversity, a better future is always possible. Combined with his drive to succeed, these lessons formed a sturdy bridge to a future he had yet to fully envision.

"Discipline is the bridge between goals and accomplishment." — Jim Rohn

Finding Discipline: The Marines and Beyond

As JD Vance approached adulthood, he stood at a crossroads. He grappled with the lingering weight of his tumultuous upbringing and the limited opportunities available in Middletown. The chaotic environment of his youth had left its mark, but it had also made him determined to rise above his circumstances. Faced with the prospect of staying trapped in the same cycle of poverty and instability that defined much of his community, Vance knew he needed a way out—a chance to transform his life. For him, that opportunity came in the form of the United States Marine Corps.

By the time Vance graduated from high school, he found himself in a familiar yet disheartening position—uncertain about his future and unsure how to break free from the constraints of his environment. While he had made strides academically, the chaos of his home life and the economic stagnation of Middletown had left him without a clear path forward. College seemed like an unattainable luxury, both financially and culturally. The idea of settling into a low-paying, dead-end job, as so many around him had done, was equally unappealing.

Vance's struggles weren't unique. Many of his peers faced similar challenges, trapped in a community where hope often felt like a scarce commodity. Addiction, unemployment, and fractured families were the backdrop of their lives, and the options for escaping that reality were few. Vance's growing frustration with this cycle of despair only deepened his resolve to forge a different path. He knew he needed something drastic—something that could provide the structure, discipline, and sense of purpose his life lacked.

Middletown was more than just a town for Vance; it was a symbol of everything he wanted to overcome. He often reflected on the struggles of those around him—the way economic decline had sapped the spirit of the community, leaving behind a sense of resignation. He saw people he cared about succumb to addiction, give up on their dreams, or simply accept a life of hardship as inevitable. These observations fueled his determination to escape, but they also left him searching for a way to channel that ambition into action.

The Marines, with their reputation for discipline, toughness, and transformation, seemed like the answer. For Vance, enlisting wasn't just about leaving Middletown; it was about proving to himself that he could be more than his circumstances. It was a decision born out of both necessity and hope, a leap into the unknown with the promise of something greater.

Vance's decision to enlist in the Marines wasn't made lightly. He knew that military life would be demanding, both physically and mentally, and that it would push him far beyond his comfort zone. But that was precisely what appealed to him. The discipline and structure of the Corps offered the opposite of the chaos of his upbringing, promising a chance to rebuild himself from the ground up.

For Vance, the Marines were, first and foremost, an opportunity for self-improvement. He wanted to prove to himself and to others that he was capable of achieving something significant and that he could rise above the limitations imposed by his past. The Corps offered a path to do just that, instilling qualities like leadership, resilience, and accountability that would serve him well in every aspect of his life.

Despite his determination, Vance faced moments of doubt and fear leading up to his enlistment. The idea of leaving Middletown, his family, and everything familiar was daunting, even if those things had caused him pain. He wondered if he was tough enough to endure the rigors of boot camp or if he would fail and find himself back where he started. These fears were compounded by the fact that military service came with its own set of risks, including the possibility of deployment to a war zone.

But Vance knew that staying in Middletown would mean accepting a life he didn't want. The fear of regret—the fear of never trying— outweighed his doubts. With that resolve, he signed the paperwork, took the oath, and prepared to embark on a journey that would change his life forever.

The decision to join the Marines sparked mixed reactions from Vance's family. Mamaw, fiercely protective as always, was both proud and apprehensive. She admired his courage and supported his desire to escape the limitations of Middletown, but the thought of Vance facing the dangers of military life worried her deeply. In typical Mamaw fashion, she didn't hold back her opinions.

Papaw, though quieter, expressed his support in his own understated way. A man who valued hard work and perseverance, he respected Vance's decision to pursue a path that demanded discipline and sacrifice. Other family members had their doubts, questioning whether Vance could handle the intensity of the Marines or if he was making the right choice. But for Vance, the decision was already made. He knew what he wanted, and he was ready to fight for it.

Vance's enlistment in the United States Marine Corps signaled the beginning of a new chapter in his life. It was a leap into the unknown, driven by a desire to escape the shadows of his past and build a brighter future. The decision wasn't easy, and the path ahead would be challenging, but it was exactly what Vance needed—a chance to prove to himself that he was capable of achieving greatness.

*   *   *

Marine Corps boot camp is widely regarded as one of the toughest training programs in the world, designed to strip away individuality and rebuild recruits into disciplined, cohesive units. For JD Vance, it was both an ordeal and a revelation. Stepping into the unforgiving world of Marine Corps training was like nothing he had ever experienced, but it was exactly the challenge he needed to unlock the potential he had always believed he possessed. Boot camp didn't just teach Vance how to be a Marine; it fundamentally reshaped his character, instilling values and skills that would serve him for a lifetime.

The moment Vance stepped off the bus at Parris Island, South Carolina, he was greeted by the thunderous bark of a drill instructor ordering him to line up and drop his bag. It was a rude awakening to the regimented, high-stakes world of Marine Corps training. The days began before dawn with the piercing sound of a bugle, followed by hours of relentless physical training, drills, and instruction. Recruits were expected to meet exacting standards at all times—beds made to perfection, uniforms spotless, and movements executed with precision.

The physical challenges were grueling. Vance, like many recruits, was pushed to his limits during obstacle courses, forced marches, and endless rounds of push-ups and sit-ups. But it was the mental toughness required to endure the constant pressure that proved the most difficult. Drill instructors knew how to find a recruit's breaking point, exploiting weaknesses to weed out those who couldn't handle the demands of the Corps. For Vance, this was a trial by fire—one that would test not just his body but his willpower.

The first weeks of boot camp were some of the hardest of Vance's life. He struggled to keep up with the pace of training and adapt to the harsh discipline imposed by the drill instructors. Simple mistakes—a missed detail during inspection, a slight delay in a drill—were met with loud reprimands and extra physical punishment. At times, he questioned whether he had made the right choice in enlisting. The chaos of boot camp felt eerily familiar, mirroring the instability of his childhood, but this time there was no escape.

Yet, Vance refused to give up. He leaned on the resilience he had developed growing up in Middletown, drawing strength from the tough lessons of his past. Each day, he focused on improving— running a little faster, listening more carefully, and pushing himself harder than he thought possible. Slowly but surely, he began to adapt, finding a rhythm in the regimented lifestyle that had once felt so foreign.

Boot camp demanded discipline at every turn, from maintaining personal appearance to executing complex drills as a unit. For Vance, this was transformative. The Marine Corps instilled in him a level of focus and attention to detail that had been missing from his life. He learned to follow orders without hesitation, understanding that success in the Corps—and in life—depended on discipline and consistency.

Equally important was the emphasis on teamwork. In boot camp, no one succeeded alone. Whether it was navigating an obstacle course or completing a field exercise, recruits had to rely on one another to achieve their objectives. Vance quickly realized that his own performance could directly impact the group, and this sense of accountability reshaped how he thought about responsibility. It wasn't just about meeting his own standards; it was about earning the trust and respect of those around him.

Perhaps the most profound lesson Vance learned in boot camp was the value of purpose. For the first time in his life, he felt part of something larger than himself—a brotherhood dedicated to service and excellence. The Marine Corps gave him a clear mission, one that required him to rise above his personal doubts and focus on contributing to the greater good. This sense of purpose, combined with the resilience he developed during training, became a cornerstone of Vance's identity.

As the weeks of boot camp went on, Vance began to notice a change in himself. Tasks that had once seemed impossible became routine, and the physical challenges he had dreaded became opportunities to prove his strength. Completing the grueling Crucible, a fifty-four-hour final exercise designed to test every skill learned during training, was a turning point. Exhausted and sleep-deprived, Vance emerged from the experience with a newfound sense of pride and confidence. He had faced one of the toughest challenges of his life and come out the other side stronger.

Throughout his time in boot camp, Vance encountered instructors and peers who pushed him to excel. One drill instructor, known for his brutal honesty and exacting standards, became a figure of both fear and inspiration. The instructor's words stayed with him, driving him to push past self-doubt and embrace his potential.

Vance also formed bonds with his fellow recruits, many of whom came from backgrounds as challenging as his own. Sharing stories during rare moments of downtime, Vance realized that he was not alone in his struggles. These relationships reminded him of the power of camaraderie and the importance of lifting each other up—a lesson he would carry with him long after boot camp.

Marine Corps boot camp forged Vance into a disciplined, confident, and resilient individual. It taught him that he could endure hardship, overcome self-doubt, and rise to meet even the most daunting challenges. The values of discipline, teamwork, and accountability became deeply ingrained, shaping not only the Marine he would become but the leader he would one day be.

*   *   *

Soon enough, Vance found himself in a world far removed from anything he had known in Middletown, Ohio. Deployed to Iraq, he experienced the arid desert landscape, the oppressive heat, and the constant tension of being in a war zone. His role as a Marine required him to adapt quickly to the challenges of this new environment, where the stakes were often life or death.

As part of a logistics unit, Vance's responsibilities ranged from ensuring the safe transport of supplies to maintaining operational readiness under difficult conditions. These tasks, while not always glamorous, were critical to the success of the broader mission. Every convoy, every shipment, and every operation carried with it the risk of ambush or attack, forcing Vance and his fellow Marines to remain vigilant at all times.

One of the defining aspects of Vance's time in Iraq was the camaraderie he built with his fellow Marines. In the face of danger and uncertainty, the bonds formed between comrades became a lifeline. Vance recalls late nights spent sharing stories, jokes, and fears with his unit, moments that offered a reprieve from the intensity of their surroundings.

These relationships transcended differences in background and upbringing. Whether from big cities or small towns, each Marine brought their own story to the unit, creating a sense of unity that was vital to their survival. Vance found that, much like his experiences with Mamaw and Papaw, loyalty and trust were the bedrock of these relationships. The men and women he served alongside became his extended family, united by a shared commitment to their mission.

Iraq presented Vance with challenges that tested his leadership and decision-making skills in ways he had never anticipated. In one instance, his unit faced a logistical dilemma while transporting essential supplies through a region known for insurgent activity. The situation required quick thinking, careful planning, and the ability to remain calm under pressure. Vance's ability to analyze the situation, weigh the risks, and make decisive choices earned him the respect of his peers and superiors.

These moments of leadership allowed Vance to take responsibility for the lives of those around him. Vance often found himself grappling with the weight of his role, knowing that the choices he made could have profound consequences for his unit. The sense of accountability he developed in Iraq would stay with him long after he left the military.

The dangers he encountered were not theoretical. Convoys came under fire, roadside bombs posed constant threats, and the unpredictable nature of the conflict kept everyone on edge. These experiences forced Vance to confront the fragility of life and the courage it took to keep moving forward in the face of fear.

One day, a close call during a routine operation could have ended in tragedy. The incident underscored the unpredictability of war and the ever-present need for vigilance. It also reinforced his gratitude for the teamwork and training that kept him and his unit alive.

Vance's time in Iraq gave him a new perspective on humanity. He saw both the best and worst of people—the bravery of his fellow Marines, the resilience of local civilians, and the devastation wrought by conflict. These experiences deepened his understanding of the complexities of human behavior, showing him how adversity could bring out both extraordinary heroism and profound suffering.

A chance interaction with an Iraqi child during a humanitarian mission was one of those moments that left a lasting impression on Vance. The child's smile, despite the hardships of living in a war-torn region, was a reminder of the universality of hope and the resilience of the human spirit, even in the most challenging circumstances.

Iraq also expanded Vance's understanding of the interconnectedness of global events and their impact on individuals. The realities of war—displacement, destruction, and loss—were no longer abstract concepts. Seeing them firsthand gave Vance a sense of urgency about the importance of leadership, service, and thoughtful decision-making.

The experience also reinforced Vance's belief in the value of resilience and adaptability. He came to see these qualities not just as personal traits but as essential tools for navigating a world full of uncertainty and challenges. This insight would later inform his approach to leadership, writing, and public service.

Vance's deployment to Iraq matured him, shaping his character, values, and worldview. The lessons he learned about discipline, teamwork, and the complexities of humanity would influence every aspect of his life moving forward. In Iraq, Vance discovered not just who he was but who he could become—a leader, a thinker, and a servant of something greater than himself.

*   *   *

One of the most transformative aspects of Vance's time in the Marines was the discipline it instilled in him. From the grueling demands of boot camp to the high-stakes environment of deployment, every moment in the Corps required focus, precision, and accountability. This discipline became a cornerstone of Vance's character, teaching him how to prioritize, manage time effectively, and approach challenges methodically.

The Marines left little room for excuses or shortcuts. Vance learned that success was earned through consistent effort and attention to detail, lessons that would later serve him well in the classroom, the boardroom, and the political arena. The rigorous structure of military life gave him the tools to turn chaos into order, a skill that proved invaluable as he navigated the complexities of his personal and professional life.

Leadership in the Marines wasn't just about giving orders—it was about earning the respect and trust of those you served with. Vance's experiences taught him the importance of leading by example, of putting the needs of the team above his own, and of making tough decisions under pressure. Whether it was organizing a convoy in Iraq or mentoring younger Marines, Vance developed a leadership style rooted in empathy, accountability, and a commitment to the mission.

Perseverance was another key lesson. The physical and mental challenges of military life pushed Vance to his limits, forcing him to confront his fears and doubts head-on. He discovered that resilience wasn't about avoiding failure but about finding the strength to keep going in the face of setbacks. This mindset became a defining trait, one that allowed him to overcome the hurdles of his childhood and the challenges that lay ahead.

Perhaps the most profound impact of Vance's time in the Marines was the sense of identity and confidence it gave him. For much of his early life, Vance had struggled to see himself as more than a product of his environment. The Marine Corps changed that. It showed him that he was capable of achieving great things, of rising above his circumstances, and of contributing to something larger than himself.

This newfound confidence enabled Vance to understand his place in the world. The Marines gave Vance a sense of purpose, a clear mission, and a community of peers who shared his values. For the first time, he felt like he belonged to something meaningful, a feeling that stayed with him long after his service ended.

The lessons Vance learned in the Marines became the foundation for how he approached challenges in every aspect of his life. Whether it was navigating the demands of higher education, writing *Hillbilly Elegy*, or running for political office, Vance drew on the discipline, resilience, and leadership skills he had developed during his military service. He understood that success wasn't about avoiding difficulty but about confronting it with clarity and determination.

This mindset was especially evident during his time at Yale Law School, where Vance often felt like an outsider among his wealthier, more privileged peers. Instead of letting those feelings hold him back, he used them as motivation to prove himself. The confidence and work ethic he had gained in the Marines gave him the tools to excel, even in an environment that felt foreign and intimidating.

The values instilled in Vance during his time in the Marines also shaped his approach to leadership in his later roles as an author, politician, and ultimately, vice president. The Marine Corps taught him the importance of accountability—not just to oneself but to the people you serve. It reinforced the idea that true leadership isn't about seeking power or recognition but about making decisions that benefit the greater good.

These principles became central to Vance political philosophy. His speeches and policies often emphasized themes of service, sacrifice, and resilience, reflecting the values he had learned in the Corps. Whether advocating for working-class families, addressing the opioid crisis, or discussing national security, Vance military background gave him a unique perspective that resonated with voters and colleagues alike.

Looking back, Vance often credits the Marine Corps as the turning point in his life—the moment when everything changed. It wasn't just the discipline or the leadership skills or even the confidence he gained; it was the realization that he had the power to shape his own destiny. The Marines taught him how to overcome adversity—and to thrive in the face of it.

*   *   *

The transition from military life to civilian life can be jarring for any veteran, and Vance was no exception. After years of living within the rigid structure of the Marine Corps—where every day was planned down to the minute and every action had a clear purpose—civilian life felt chaotic and disorienting. Gone were the routines, the camaraderie of his fellow Marines, and the shared sense of mission. In their place was a new reality that felt both liberating and unsettling.

Returning from the structured, high-stakes environment of the Marine Corps to the relative calm of civilian life was both a relief and a challenge. While his time in the military had equipped him with discipline, resilience, and a deep sense of purpose, reintegration into a world far removed from the front lines of Iraq proved to be a complicated journey. It was a transition marked by moments of uncertainty, reflection, and ultimately, a renewed focus on education as the next step in his quest to build a better future.

Vance struggled with the absence of the discipline and accountability that had defined his military experience. The stakes of everyday life felt lower, but that lack of urgency left him searching for direction. Without the structure of the Corps to guide him, Vance found himself confronting questions about his identity and purpose: Who was he outside of the uniform? What did he want to do with his life? These were questions he hadn't had the time or space to fully consider while in the Marines, but they loomed large now.

Beyond the logistical challenges of reintegration, Vance also grappled with the emotional aftermath of his time in Iraq. The experiences he had on deployment—both the moments of danger and the quieter, more reflective ones—stayed with him. He often found himself replaying scenes from his time overseas, reflecting on the lessons he had learned and the sacrifices he had witnessed.

There were moments of guilt and self-doubt, common among veterans returning from war. Vance wondered if he had done enough, if he had made the right choices, and how his service fit into the larger narrative of his life. These reflections were both a burden and a motivator, pushing him to find ways to honor his experiences by making the most of the opportunities ahead.

Reintegrating into a non-military environment also meant figuring out how to navigate relationships and responsibilities in a world that felt fundamentally different from the one he had left. Vance's family and friends had continued their lives while he was away, and reconnecting with them wasn't always easy. He carried with him a perspective shaped by war and discipline, one that didn't always align with the experiences of those around him.

Despite these challenges, Vance approached reintegration with the same determination that had carried him through boot camp and Iraq. He understood that this was yet another test of his resilience, one that required him to apply the lessons he had learned in the Marines to a new and unfamiliar context.

Amid the challenges of reintegration, Vance found a sense of clarity in his decision to pursue higher education. College had always seemed like a distant dream during his childhood, an unattainable goal for someone from his background. But the confidence and discipline he had developed in the Marines gave him the tools to believe it was possible—and the GI Bill provided him with the financial means to make it a reality.

Vance chose Ohio State University as the starting point for his academic journey. It was a decision rooted in pragmatism and ambition: OSU was close enough to home to feel familiar, but it also offered a world of opportunities beyond what he had known in Middletown. Higher education was a means of breaking free from the limitations of his past and opening doors to a future he could barely imagine.

The habits Vance had developed in the Marines served him well in the classroom. He approached his studies with the same rigor and focus that had carried him through boot camp and deployment. Time management, attention to detail, and the ability to perform under pressure became his greatest assets, allowing him to excel academically even in subjects that initially intimidated him.

Vance also brought a unique perspective to his education. His time in the military had given him a global view of issues and a firsthand understanding of the complexities of leadership, service, and resilience. These experiences enriched his interactions with professors and classmates, allowing him to contribute insights that went beyond textbooks and lectures.

For Vance, college was a time when he could find his sense of purpose. Each class, each paper, and each conversation with a mentor reinforced his belief that education was the key to unlocking a better future. It was during this time that he began to see himself not just as a survivor of his circumstances but as someone capable of shaping his own destiny.

His time at Ohio State equipped him with both the skills and the confidence to pursue even greater ambitions. It was a period of growth and self-discovery, one that set the stage for his eventual journey to Yale Law School and beyond.

Vance approached college life with the same sense of purpose and determination that had carried him through boot camp and deployment. Unlike many of his peers, who were still adjusting to the newfound freedom of college, Vance thrived in the structured environment he created for himself. He built a routine that prioritized his studies, treating his academic responsibilities with the seriousness of a military mission.

His days were meticulously organized: early mornings spent reviewing notes, afternoons in class or at the library, and evenings dedicated to preparing for the next day. This discipline allowed Vance to stay ahead in his coursework, even in challenging subjects that might have intimidated him otherwise. He wasn't just there to pass classes—he was there to excel, knowing that his success at Ohio State was a crucial step toward the life he envisioned.

Despite his determination, adapting to college life wasn't without its challenges. Vance often felt out of place among his classmates, many of whom came from more privileged backgrounds. The cultural divide between his working-class roots and the academic environment of Ohio State sometimes left him questioning whether he truly belonged. But rather than letting these doubts hold him back, Vance used them as motivation to prove himself.

He stayed focused on his long-term goals, constantly reminding himself of why he was there: to build a future that he could be proud of.

At Ohio State, the influence of professors who recognized his potential and encouraged him to push himself further was key to his growth. In one political science course, a professor took note of his sharp analytical skills and engaged him in discussions about policy and governance. Their conversations sparked Vance's interest in public policy, helping him see how his own experiences could inform his understanding of broader societal issues.

Peers also played a critical role in Vance's growth. He found a sense of camaraderie with students who shared his drive and determination. Group projects, late-night study sessions, and debates in the classroom exposed Vance to new perspectives and challenged him to refine his ideas.

It was during his time at Ohio State that Vance first began to consider a career in law and public policy. A class on constitutional law, in particular, opened his eyes to the ways in which legal systems shape society. The course's focus on justice, governance, and the role of the individual in a democratic system resonated deeply with Vance, reminding him of the struggles he had witnessed growing up in Middletown.

Through these academic experiences, Vance began to see a path forward—not just as a student but as someone who could use his education to make a tangible difference in the world. He started to envision a career where he could advocate for those who, like him, had been shaped by the challenges of poverty and instability. This realization became the driving force behind his decision to apply to law school, a choice that would ultimately change the trajectory of his life.

Ohio State University catalyzed a period of profound growth and self-discovery. The influence of mentors, the camaraderie of peers, and his growing passion for law and public policy all contributed to a sense of momentum that propelled Vance forward. He began to see the full scope of what was possible and laid the groundwork for his next great leap—a journey into the elite and often intimidating world of Yale Law School.

"Education is the most powerful weapon which you can use to change the world." — Nelson Mandela

The Yale Years

For JD Vance, Yale Law School was an entirely new world far from his roots in Middletown, Ohio. Gaining admission to one of the most elite law schools in the country was a triumph, but it also posed its own set of challenges. For a man shaped by the hard realities of working-class America, stepping into the hallowed halls of Yale represented both an opportunity to refine his ambitions and a test of his ability to thrive in a space so far removed from the life he had known.

Vance's decision to apply to Yale was bold and deliberate, the culmination of years spent preparing himself for something greater. His time in the Marines had instilled in him the discipline and confidence to take risks, while his academic success at Ohio State University gave him the tools to believe he could compete with the best and brightest. But applying to Yale wasn't just about ambition; it was about bridging a divide. Vance saw Yale as a gateway to the corridors of power—law firms, courts, and policy circles where decisions were made and futures were shaped.

For Vance, attending Yale was an opportunity to bring his unique working-class perspective into a space that rarely heard voices like his. It was a chance to challenge the stereotypes surrounding people from

Appalachia and show that their struggles and resilience were just as relevant to the national conversation as the experiences of the privileged elite.

The gulf between Middletown and Yale could not have been wider. Where Middletown had been defined by economic decline, addiction, and a fight for survival, Yale epitomized success, stability, and influence. The ornate buildings, manicured lawns, and air of intellectual sophistication stood in stark contrast to the steel mills and modest homes of Vance's hometown. For someone who had grown up with a deep awareness of what it meant to be an outsider, stepping into this environment was both exhilarating and intimidating.

Later, he reflected that social mobility happened when there was a lifestyle change. A different set of norms and mores applied to this set, and he began to realize it at Yale.

Vance often reflected on how out of place he felt during those early days. His classmates came from backgrounds that seemed worlds apart from his own—sons and daughters of lawyers, bankers, and academics, many of whom had attended elite private schools. Their ease with the unspoken rules of the Ivy League only heightened Vance's sense of alienation. Yale immersed him into a culture he barely understood.

The moment when Vance received his acceptance letter was surreal. It was the culmination of years of hard work and determination, but it also came with a heavy dose of self-doubt. He wondered if he truly belonged among the nation's top law students, many of whom had enjoyed advantages he could scarcely imagine. Imposter syndrome crept in, threatening to overshadow the excitement of his achievement.

But beneath the doubts was a steely determination. Vance had overcome too much to let insecurity hold him back now. Mamaw's voice rang in his head: "Don't you dare let anyone make you feel like you don't belong." With her words as a constant reminder, Vance resolved to prove that he was more than capable of thriving at Yale— not just for himself, but for the people and places he represented.

Vance's admission to Yale Law School was a turning point, marking the beginning of a chapter that would test him in ways he had never experienced before. It was a chance to refine his skills, expand his worldview, and find his voice in a space that often overlooked people like him. While the challenges ahead were daunting, Vance approached them with the same resilience and determination that had carried him through boot camp, Iraq, and Ohio State.

As Vance prepared to step into this new world, he carried with him the lessons of his past: the discipline of the Marines, the encouragement of mentors, and the belief that his story mattered. In the chapters that followed, Yale would become not just a proving ground for his intellect but the place where he would forge his identity, learning to navigate the complexities of elite culture while staying true to his roots.

Yale Law School was a dream realized for Vance, but it thrust him into a world that felt foreign and, at times, unwelcoming. For a working-class student from Middletown, Ohio, the transition into one of the most elite institutions in the country came with its share of obstacles—cultural, financial, and social. These challenges, however, became opportunities for growth.

From the moment Vance stepped onto the Yale campus, the differences between his working-class upbringing and the privileged environment of his new peers became glaringly apparent. At Middletown High School, conversations revolved around factory layoffs, local sports, and scraping by. At Yale, his classmates casually discussed summer internships at top law firms, family vacations to Europe, and connections to influential figures.

Vance often found himself at a loss in these conversations, unsure how to respond or relate. One particularly jarring moment came during a discussion about spring break plans. While his peers debated whether to go skiing in Aspen or relax on a Caribbean island, Vance quietly reflected on the fact that his vacations growing up often meant staying home because his family couldn't afford to travel. The dissonance between their realities and his left him feeling out of place, but it also fueled his determination to prove that his background didn't make him any less capable.

Beyond wealth, Yale's culture of networking and social polish was another challenge for Vance. His classmates seemed fluent in the unspoken rules of elite academia, from effortlessly navigating cocktail parties to leveraging familial connections to secure coveted opportunities. Vance, on the other hand, was still learning how to present himself in these settings. Small talk at networking events felt stilted, and the idea of asking for help or guidance from professors and peers felt foreign, even intimidating.

Yet, Vance's outsider perspective also became a strength. While he initially struggled to find common ground with his classmates, he began to realize that his unique experiences offered a valuable perspective that many of them lacked. Slowly, he learned to navigate this unfamiliar world without compromising his authenticity, finding ways to bring his voice and story into the conversation.

The financial realities of attending Yale Law School were another hurdle for Vance. While many of his peers came from families who could afford to support their education, Vance relied on a combination of scholarships, student loans, and his savings from the Marines to cover tuition and living expenses. Even with this support, the cost of living in New Haven, combined with the demands of law school, required careful budgeting and sacrifices.

Vance's lifestyle at Yale was frugal by necessity. While some classmates dined at upscale restaurants, he cooked simple meals at home. When others splurged on suits for interviews, Vance made do with what he could afford, carefully ironing and maintaining his limited wardrobe. These small acts of resourcefulness became a point of pride for him, a reminder of the values instilled by Mamaw and Papaw—making the most of what you have and never wasting an opportunity.

Socially, Yale presented Vance with a delicate balancing act. He wanted to connect with his classmates and build relationships that would help him succeed in law school and beyond, but he also wanted to remain true to his working-class roots. This tension often left him feeling like he was living in two worlds, neither of which fully understood the other.

One of Vance's early missteps came during a group discussion on career goals. While many of his peers confidently shared their aspirations to work at prestigious law firms or clerk for Supreme Court justices, Vance hesitated to voice his own ambitions, worried that his background might make him seem less polished or capable. It took time for him to realize that his story—of resilience, grit, and service—was not a liability but an asset.

Despite these challenges, Vance gradually found ways to connect with his classmates. Some were genuinely curious about his background and the perspective he brought to discussions. Others admired his ability to balance ambition with authenticity, seeing in him a determination that transcended social and economic divides. Over time, Vance built meaningful relationships, both personal and professional, that would become invaluable as he moved forward in his career.

While Yale Law School challenged Vance in ways he hadn't expected, it also gave him the opportunity to refine his identity and find his footing in an elite environment. The cultural shock, financial struggles, and social adjustments he faced were not just obstacles—they were opportunities to grow, to learn, and to prove that his working-class roots were a source of strength, not a barrier.

While Yale Law School was a challenging and often intimidating environment, it was also a place of tremendous growth. Guided by key mentors, inspired by formative experiences, and shaped by the lessons he learned in the classroom, Vance began to see how his personal story and professional ambitions could intersect. These years were about more than learning the law—they were about finding his voice, building confidence, and solidifying his goals for the future.

Mentorship played a pivotal role in Vance's time at Yale. Early in his first year, he crossed paths with a professor who quickly became one of his greatest advocates. This mentor, a celebrated legal scholar with a deep interest in issues of inequality and systemic injustice, saw something in Vance that many others missed—a unique perspective shaped by his working-class roots and military service.

The professor encouraged Vance to draw on his personal experiences to inform his academic work, showing him how his story could add depth and authenticity to his legal arguments. This guidance helped Vance realize that his background was a strength.

Another key figure in Vance's journey was an alumni mentor who worked in public interest law. During a networking event, this individual shared stories of using the law to advocate for underserved communities, sparking Vance's interest in how legal frameworks could be used to create tangible change. Their conversations inspired Vance to think more broadly about how he could use his legal education to address the challenges facing working-class Americans.

Under the guidance of these mentors, Vance began to explore how his personal story could connect with his professional ambitions. He started to see his journey as a lens through which he could approach complex legal and social issues. Whether it was addressing the opioid crisis, advocating for economic opportunity, or analyzing the role of law in perpetuating inequality, Vance's mentors helped him recognize that his voice could be a powerful tool for change.

Academically, Vance's coursework at Yale challenged him in ways he hadn't anticipated. Classes like Constitutional Law and Public Policy introduced him to the complexities of governance and justice, while seminars on poverty law and economic disparity resonated deeply with his own experiences. In one particularly memorable lecture, a professor posed a question about the role of the judiciary in addressing systemic inequality. For Vance, the discussion felt personal—he wasn't just grappling with abstract legal theories; he was thinking about the families back in Middletown who bore the brunt of these issues.

These moments in the classroom provided opportunities for Vance to connect his studies to the real world. He began to see how the legal concepts he was learning could be applied to address the challenges he had witnessed growing up, from addiction and unemployment to the erosion of social mobility.

Like many of his peers, Vance found some aspects of law school daunting. The Socratic method, with its rapid-fire questioning, could be unnerving, and the dense legal texts often felt far removed from his everyday reality. But Vance's resilience and work ethic carried him through. He stayed up late poring over case law, sought out study groups for support, and wasn't afraid to ask questions when he didn't understand something.

Over time, Vance discovered that his practical perspective often added value to classroom discussions. While some classmates approached the material from purely theoretical standpoints, Vance's lived experience allowed him to bring a grounded, real-world lens to the table. This realization boosted his confidence and reinforced his belief that he belonged at Yale.

Outside the classroom, JD pursued internships and projects that pushed him out of his comfort zone and deepened his understanding of the legal profession. One summer, he worked at a prominent law firm where he was exposed to high-stakes cases involving corporate clients and complex litigation. While the work was demanding, Vance excelled, impressing his supervisors with his ability to think critically and work under pressure.

In another internship, Vance had the chance to work on a pro bono case that involved advocating for a family. The experience was a stark reminder of the issues he had seen in Middletown and underscored the importance of using the law to protect vulnerable populations. It was during this time that Vance began to think seriously about how he could balance a successful legal career with his desire to give back to the communities he cared about.

One of the most pivotal moments of Vance's time at Yale came during a moot court competition. Assigned to argue a complex case in front of a panel of professors and alumni, Vance initially felt overwhelmed by the task. But as he prepared, he realized how far he had come—from the chaos of his childhood to the disciplined focus of the Marines to the intellectual rigor of Yale. When the day of the competition arrived, Vance delivered a powerful and well-reasoned argument, earning praise from the judges and admiration from his peers.

This moment affirmed that Vance could not only survive in this elite environment but thrive in it. For the first time, he fully embraced his place at Yale, recognizing his background and experiences as unique assets he could leverage for success.

*   *   *

As Vance navigated life at Yale, he couldn't help but notice how privilege shaped his classmates' opportunities and outlooks. Many of his peers had grown up in families where college was a given, where connections to powerful networks were passed down like heirlooms, and where failure was cushioned by financial security. For them, Yale was a natural extension of their lives—a prestigious stepping stone, but not an insurmountable challenge.

Vance often observed how this privilege manifested in subtle but significant ways. Classmates spoke confidently about career opportunities, relying on their parents' connections to land internships at top law firms. They discussed summer trips abroad or high-level extracurricular activities that had padded their résumés long before they applied to law school. For Vance, who had relied on the GI Bill to fund his education and whose path to Yale had been anything but linear, these experiences underscored the systemic advantages that many of his peers took for granted.

Vance's observations of privilege were a step forward in recognizing the systemic barriers that kept people like him out of elite institutions. He reflected on how the economic and cultural realities of working-class life often made higher education seem unattainable. From the underfunded schools in places like Middletown to the lack of mentors who could guide students toward ambitious goals, the deck often felt stacked against those from his background.

These reflections deepened Vance's understanding of inequality and the structural forces that perpetuate it. He saw how the American education system, while often touted as a meritocratic pathway to success, was riddled with inequities that made it far easier for some to climb the ladder than others. These realizations would later shape his critiques of both political parties and their approaches to addressing class divides.

Despite the stark disparities he witnessed, Vance's experience at Yale reinforced his belief in the transformative power of education. He understood, perhaps better than most, that education had been the key to his own escape from poverty. The opportunities he had gained through his time at Ohio State and Yale were proof that, for those who managed to navigate the barriers, education could still be a powerful equalizer.

But Vance also grappled with difficult questions about whether the American Dream was truly accessible to everyone. Sitting in classrooms surrounded by privilege, he couldn't ignore the fact that his own journey was the exception, not the rule. He often wondered how many others like him—intelligent, hardworking, and full of potential—were held back by circumstances beyond their control. These reflections added complexity to his views on meritocracy, leaving him both inspired by his own success and troubled by the systemic inequities that made stories like his so rare.

One of Vance's most important moments of reflection came during a conversation with a classmate who dismissed the struggles of the working class as a matter of personal failure. The comment stung, not because it was uncommon— Vance had encountered similar attitudes before—but because it crystallized the divide between those who had lived through hardship and those who viewed it from a distance.

In that moment, Vance realized how deeply his own experiences shaped his perspective. Beyond his role as a student Yale, he was a representative of a world that was often invisible in elite spaces. This realization reinforced his belief that education and opportunity should not be reserved for the privileged few but made accessible to all.

Vance's experiences at Yale deepened his resolve to address inequality. He began to see his legal education not just as a personal achievement but as a tool to give voice to the struggles of the working class. Whether in classroom discussions, internships, or informal conversations, Vance made it a point to bring the realities of places like Middletown into the room, challenging assumptions and pushing for a broader understanding of the American experience.

This commitment wasn't always easy. Vance often felt like he was straddling two worlds—one that demanded he assimilate into the culture of privilege and another that called him to stay true to his roots. But rather than seeing this tension as a weakness, Vance began to view it as a strength. His ability to navigate both spaces gave him a unique perspective, one that he hoped to use to bridge the divide between them.

By the time Vance graduated from Yale, his experiences had solidified his vision for the future. He saw his story not just as a testament to resilience but as a platform to advocate for those who had been left behind. Whether through writing, public speaking, or policy work, Vance was determined to use his voice to highlight the challenges facing working-class Americans and to push for solutions that addressed the root causes of inequality.

Vance's time at Yale Law School was a study in contrasts—privilege and poverty, opportunity and inequity, ambition and doubt. It was a period of profound growth, one that forced him to confront difficult truths about the American Dream while reaffirming his commitment to making it more attainable for others.

*   *   *

Graduating from Yale was an achievement Vance could scarcely have imagined during his tumultuous upbringing in Middletown, Ohio. As he walked across the stage to receive his diploma, he reflected on the long journey that had brought him to this moment: the discipline instilled in him by the Marines, the grit that carried him through Ohio State, and the resilience that helped him find his footing in the elite world of Yale.

While the moment was one of pride, it was also deeply humbling. Vance knew how rare his story was and how many others from places like Middletown never had the opportunities he was afforded. This realization fueled a sense of responsibility to use his education and platform to advocate for those whose voices were often overlooked.

Vance's thoughts also turned to the mentors and peers who had supported him during his time at Yale. Professors who encouraged him to see his background as a strength, classmates who challenged him to think differently, and alumni who opened doors to career opportunities—all had played a role in shaping his journey. Their belief in his potential had often buoyed him during moments of doubt, reminding him that he belonged at Yale and that his voice mattered.

Vance felt a deep sense of gratitude for the lessons learned outside the classroom. Yale had forced him to confront questions about privilege, class, and opportunity, challenging him to reconcile his working-class roots with the world of power and influence he now inhabited. These lessons weren't just academic—they were personal, and they would inform his decisions and leadership style in the years to come.

Graduating from Yale would take him into the worlds of business, writing, and eventually politics. Armed with a law degree from one of the nation's most prestigious institutions, Vance was poised to enter the professional sphere with confidence and credibility.

Preston D. Munro

"A wise man will make more opportunities than he finds."
— Francis Bacon

Into the Professional World

JD Vance's professional journey is as unconventional as it is influential. Before becoming a bestselling author and a political figure, Vance carved a path through some of the most elite institutions in law, finance, and venture capital. His career after Yale Law School and before *Hillbilly Elegy* consisted of a series of roles that would shape his worldview, his understanding of economic systems, and ultimately, his approach to public service.

From his early experiences in corporate law, where he gained insight into the legal and regulatory frameworks of major businesses, to his transition into venture capital, where he evaluated and invested in startups, Vance's career choices reflected a deep curiosity about how industries function and how wealth is created—and sometimes lost—in America. Each step in his journey informed his perspective on the country's economic landscape and the disparities between the prosperous urban elite and struggling rural communities like the one he came from.

His time in Silicon Valley exposed him to the rapid pace of technological innovation and the immense capital that fueled it, while his work in venture capital underscored the power of investment in shaping industries and communities. Unlike many who enter finance purely for personal gain, Vance saw these experiences as a way to better understand the economic forces shaping America's future.

As he moved between these different worlds—law, finance, and technology—Vance carried with him the lessons of his Appalachian upbringing. He sought to bridge the gap between the elites of the corporate world and the blue-collar communities that had been left behind by globalization and economic shifts. His professional trajectory was not just about building a résumé; it was about building a philosophy—one that would eventually guide his writing, his politics, and his leadership.

*   *   *

After graduating from Yale Law School in 2013, JD Vance embarked on a legal career that would provide him with a deep understanding of the judicial system, legislative processes, and corporate law. Unlike many of his peers who pursued high-profile law firm careers in Washington, D.C., or New York, Vance's early professional choices reflected his desire to gain exposure to different branches of the legal world. His experiences as a judicial clerk, legislative staffer, and corporate attorney helped shape his views on law, governance, and economic regulation—perspectives that would later influence his work in venture capital and, ultimately, his approach to policymaking.

Vance's first major legal role after Yale was clerking for Judge David Bunning in the U.S. District Court for the Eastern District of

Kentucky. Judge Bunning, a George W. Bush appointee, was best known for presiding over politically sensitive cases, including the widely publicized ruling against Kentucky county clerk Kim Davis for refusing to issue marriage licenses to same-sex couples. As a law clerk, Vance was responsible for conducting legal research, drafting opinions, and assisting with the interpretation of complex federal statutes. The role exposed him to the mechanics of federal trial courts, from evidentiary rulings to constitutional law disputes. It was here that Vance gained firsthand experience in how legal principles shaped real-world cases—an education that would later inform his perspectives on the role of the judiciary in American democracy.

Seeking exposure beyond the courtroom, Vance transitioned to legislative work, joining the office of U.S. Senator John Cornyn (R-TX). Cornyn, a senior Republican on the Senate Judiciary Committee, played a key role in judicial nominations, federal sentencing reform, and national security legislation. Working in Cornyn's office introduced Vance to the intersection of law and politics, where legal philosophy met the practical realities of governance. His responsibilities included analyzing policy proposals, researching judicial appointments, and drafting briefings on issues ranging from regulatory oversight to criminal justice reform. The experience provided him with an insider's perspective on how Congress influences the judiciary—from shaping the composition of the Supreme Court to enacting laws that define the boundaries of corporate and individual freedoms.

While Vance found the intellectual engagement of legal work fulfilling, he soon shifted his focus to corporate law, joining Sidley Austin, one of the nation's most prestigious law firms. At Sidley, Vance specialized in corporate transactions, mergers and acquisitions, and regulatory compliance—areas of law that governed the financial operations of major businesses. His work involved advising companies on structuring deals, navigating complex business regulations, and mitigating legal risks. For a young attorney, Sidley Austin offered a lucrative and influential career path, providing access to high-stakes corporate negotiations and major financial institutions.

However, despite the prestige and financial stability that came with working at a top law firm, Vance quickly realized that corporate law was not where he wanted to build his future. The day-to-day reality of legal practice—long hours spent poring over contracts, drafting regulatory filings, and negotiating business deals—felt disconnected from the issues he truly cared about: economic mobility, job creation, and the long-term structural challenges facing working-class communities like his own in Ohio. His interest lay not in legal technicalities but in the economic forces that shaped industries, determined wages, and dictated whether communities thrived or declined.

After spending less than two years in corporate law, Vance made the decision to leave the field altogether. He had gained valuable insights into how businesses functioned, how financial systems operated, and how legal frameworks influenced corporate decision-making, but he was eager to apply that knowledge in a more direct and impactful way. Instead of continuing on a traditional legal trajectory, he set his sights on a different arena—one that would bring him into the fast-paced world of technology and venture capital. His decision to pivot away from law was not a rejection of his legal education but rather a realization that he wanted to be at the center of economic and technological transformation rather than advising companies from the sidelines.

His next move would take him to Silicon Valley, where he would immerse himself in the world of startup investment, emerging technology, and the high-risk, high-reward landscape of venture capital. In making this transition, Vance was stepping into a world of innovation, disruption, and economic reinvention—a world that would define the next chapter of his career.

*　　*　　*

In 2016, JD Vance transitioned from corporate law to the venture capital sphere, joining Mithril Capital Management as a principal. Co-founded in 2012 by renowned investor Peter Thiel and Ajay Royan, Mithril was established to focus on growth-stage technology companies poised to transform their industries. The firm's name, inspired by a fictional metal from J.R.R. Tolkien's works, reflects its commitment to enduring value and innovation.

At Mithril, Vance was involved in evaluating and nurturing tech startups, gaining exposure to Silicon Valley's dynamic innovation ecosystem. His role encompassed identifying promising companies that leveraged technology to address significant market needs, particularly in sectors long overdue for change. This experience provided Vance with a comprehensive understanding of the challenges and opportunities inherent in scaling emerging technologies within competitive markets.

Despite the potential for impactful work, Vance's tenure at Mithril was relatively brief, lasting approximately one year. During this period, some colleagues noted his limited presence in the office, with one individual recalling, "In the year Vance was there, he never once saw him in the office."

This short stint, however, was instrumental in shaping Vance's perspective on venture capital and the tech industry, influencing his subsequent endeavors in investment and public service.

Following his time at Mithril, Vance continued his venture capital career by joining Revolution LLC, an investment firm founded by former AOL CEO Steve Case. At Revolution, Vance played a pivotal role in the "Rise of the Rest" initiative, which focuses on investing in startups located outside traditional tech hubs, aiming to drive economic growth in underserved regions.

This move aligned with Vance's commitment to fostering innovation and economic development in areas often overlooked by mainstream venture capital.

*   *   *

In March 2017, JD Vance joined Revolution LLC, an investment firm founded by Steve Case, the co-founder of AOL. Revolution focuses on funding entrepreneurs who are transforming legacy industries with innovative products and services, particularly those based outside the traditional tech hubs of New York City, San Francisco, and Boston.

At Revolution, Vance was appointed to lead the "Rise of the Rest" initiative, a program launched by Case in 2014 to promote investments in startups located in underserved regions across the United States. The initiative's mission is to drive economic growth in these areas by supporting local entrepreneurs and highlighting the potential of emerging startup ecosystems beyond the coastal tech centers.

Vance's role involved sourcing and vetting seed-stage investment opportunities, educating investors about the prospects in up-and-coming startup cities, and participating in nationwide tours to meet with founders, investors, and community leaders. His efforts aimed to bridge the gap between overlooked regions and the venture capital community, fostering innovation and job creation in areas often neglected by traditional investors.

Under Vance's leadership, the Rise of the Rest initiative gained significant momentum, culminating in the launch of a $150 million seed fund in December 2017. This fund attracted investments from high-profile individuals such as Jeff Bezos, Ray Dalio, and Meg Whitman, underscoring a growing recognition of the potential residing in America's heartland.

Vance's tenure at Revolution lasted approximately a year and a half. During this period, he played a pivotal role in accelerating the awareness and impact of the Rise of the Rest initiative, contributing to the broader mission of democratizing access to capital and fostering entrepreneurial growth across the nation.

In early 2019, Vance departed from Revolution to establish his own venture capital firm, Narya Capital, based in Ohio. This move aligned with his ongoing commitment to support startups in the Midwest and other underserved regions, continuing the work he had advanced during his time with the Rise of the Rest initiative.

Vance's efforts with Revolution and the Rise of the Rest initiative have been instrumental in shifting the venture capital community's focus toward the vast, underrepresented entrepreneurial talent spread across the United States, fostering economic revitalization in regions beyond the traditional tech corridors.

Vance's experiences at Mithril and Revolution not only expanded his investment acumen but also reinforced his dedication to bridging the gap between Silicon Valley and America's heartland, advocating for a more inclusive approach to technological advancement and economic opportunity.

*   *   *

In 2019, JD Vance co-founded Narya Capital, a Cincinnati-based venture capital firm, alongside former Mithril colleague Colin Greenspon. The firm was established with a mission to invest in early-stage startups, particularly those located in the Midwest, aiming to bridge the gap between coastal tech hubs and America's heartland. The name "Narya" is a nod to one of the "rings of power" in J.R.R. Tolkien's The Lord of the Rings, reflecting the founders' vision of empowering entrepreneurs to bring transformative change.

Narya Capital attracted significant backing from prominent figures in the tech industry, including Peter Thiel, Eric Schmidt, and Marc Andreessen. The firm's inaugural fund raised $120 million, with a strategy focused on addressing America's most pressing challenges through technological and scientific innovation. Narya's portfolio encompasses a diverse range of companies, such as:

- AppHarvest: An indoor farming company based in Kentucky, aiming to revolutionize agriculture through sustainable practices.
- Rumble: A video-sharing platform that has gained popularity as an alternative to mainstream sites, emphasizing free speech.
- Hallow: A Catholic meditation and prayer app designed to integrate faith into daily life.

- True Anomaly: A space technology company developing advanced defense capabilities.
- AmplifyBio: A biotech firm focused on accelerating the development of advanced therapies.

Narya's approach is characterized by its commitment to fostering innovation in regions often overlooked by traditional venture capital. By supporting startups in the Midwest and other underserved areas, the firm aims to stimulate economic revitalization and address systemic challenges through entrepreneurial solutions. This strategy not only provides capital but also leverages a network of experienced investors and industry leaders to mentor and guide emerging companies.

JD Vance's involvement with Narya Capital extended until his transition into public service. He took a partial leave of absence in 2021 during his Senate campaign and fully departed from the firm upon his election in 2022. Despite his exit, Narya continues to build upon the foundation he helped establish, maintaining its focus on empowering entrepreneurs and fostering innovation beyond traditional tech corridors.

Through Narya Capital, Vance sought to translate his venture capital experience into tangible economic development, aligning investment strategies with a broader vision of national renewal and regional empowerment. This endeavor reflects his belief in the potential of entrepreneurship to drive societal progress and his commitment to bridging the economic divide between America's coasts and its heartland.

But let's not get ahead of ourselves. At the same time Vance was immersed in his early law and business career, he started the process of writing *Hillbilly Elegy*, the 2016 memoir that would introduce his story to the world and spark a national conversation about the struggles of working-class Americans.

"If you want to change the world, pick up your pen and write."
— Martin Luther

Writing *Hillbilly Elegy*

If there was any one thing that catapulted JD Vance to the spotlight, it was the publication of his memoir, *Hillbilly Elegy*, in 2016, and its subsequent film adaptation in 2020. For Vance, writing *Hillbilly Elegy* was a mission. The book represented his effort to make sense of his own turbulent upbringing while shedding light on the struggles of a region and a class often ignored in national conversations. Born from a mix of personal catharsis and a broader cultural critique, *Hillbilly Elegy* sought to bridge two disparate worlds: the working-class life Vance had lived and the elite spaces he now inhabited.

The idea for *Hillbilly Elegy* began to take shape as Vance reflected on his journey from Middletown, Ohio, to Yale Law School. Writing became a way for him to process the complexities of his past—his mother's addiction, the instability of his childhood, and the resilience of figures like Mamaw and Papaw. These memories, though often painful, provided Vance with a lens to explore the broader challenges facing working-class communities.

But the book wasn't just about personal reflection. Vance felt a deep sense of responsibility to share a perspective he believed was missing from the national discourse. While many discussions about poverty and inequality focused on urban environments, the struggles of rural and small-town America—particularly those of Appalachia—were often overlooked. Vance wanted to give a voice to these experiences, hoping to spark conversations about the systemic and cultural issues that defined life in places like Middletown.

Vance began working on *Hillbilly Elegy* during a time of deep economic and social turmoil in America. The opioid epidemic was devastating families across the country, unemployment rates in post-industrial towns were climbing, and rural communities were feeling increasingly disconnected from the political and cultural centers of power. These trends weren't just statistics to Vance —they were realities he had lived through and seen firsthand.

The political landscape further underscored the urgency of his project. As populist movements gained traction and the 2016 presidential election exposed deep cultural divides, Vance recognized the importance of helping readers understand the forces driving the frustrations of working-class Americans. His book would not only tell his personal story but also provide insight into the broader societal forces shaping his community.

What made Vance's voice so compelling was his ability to bridge the gap between two vastly different worlds. As someone who had grown up in a family marked by poverty, addiction, and instability, Vance understood the struggles of working-class Americans on a deeply personal level. But his experiences at Yale and in the Marines had also given him access to elite institutions and a broader understanding of the systems that shaped society.

This dual perspective allowed Vance to approach his story with both empathy and critical distance. He wasn't content to simply recount his experiences; he wanted to analyze them, connecting his personal narrative to larger cultural and economic trends. In doing so, he hoped to create a book that was both deeply personal and universally resonant.

From the outset, Vance envisioned *Hillbilly Elegy* as more than a memoir. While the book would center on his own experiences, it would also serve as a critique of the cultural and systemic factors that contributed to the struggles of communities like his. Vance wanted to explore the intersection of personal responsibility and structural inequality, challenging readers to consider how both individual choices and societal forces shaped outcomes.

Vance's goal wasn't to provide easy answers or solutions but to spark a conversation. He believed that by sharing his story, he could help readers from different backgrounds understand the complexities of working-class life and the resilience of the people who lived it. At the same time, he hoped to challenge stereotypes about Appalachia, showing that its people were more than the caricatures often depicted in media and politics. Vance set out to write a book that would catalyze discussions, challenge assumptions, and bring attention to the realities of life in rural and small-town America.

As Vance began to write *Hillbilly Elegy*, he faced the complex challenge of intertwining his deeply personal narrative with a broader analysis of the cultural and systemic forces affecting Appalachia and working-class America. The book was never meant to be a purely autobiographical recounting of his life, nor was it solely a sociopolitical critique. Instead, Vance sought to walk a delicate line—

using his story as both a lens and a platform to explore the struggles, resilience, and failures of his community.

One of the most difficult decisions Vance made while writing *Hillbilly Elegy* was to share the intimate details of his family's struggles. Writing about his mother's battle with addiction, his grandparents' tumultuous marriage, and his own moments of despair required a level of vulnerability that few are willing to expose to the public. Vance understood the weight of these revelations—not just for himself, but for his family. Would they see his candor as betrayal or as an effort to shed light on larger issues?

Despite these concerns, Vance felt compelled to include these stories. His mother's addiction, for instance, was just one example of the opioid epidemic ravaging communities like Middletown. His grandparents' volatile yet stabilizing presence in his life illustrated the complex role that family plays in both perpetuating and overcoming hardship. These personal accounts weren't included for shock value; they were essential to painting an honest picture of the challenges facing working-class families.

Writing the book was a deeply emotional journey. Revisiting his childhood forced Vance to confront memories he had long tried to suppress: the chaos of his home life, the fear of losing his mother to addiction, and the moments of anger and guilt that still lingered. There were days when the process felt overwhelming, as though he were reliving the trauma instead of simply recounting it.

Yet, Vance also found moments of clarity and healing in the process. Writing allowed him to untangle the complicated emotions tied to his upbringing, helping him better understand the forces that shaped his family and his community. While the process was painful, it reinforced Vance's belief in the importance of telling his story—not just for himself, but for others who might see their own struggles reflected in his words.

Vance's family became the focal point of his broader critique of Appalachia and working-class America. By sharing their story, he provided readers with a human face to the statistics and headlines that often define discussions about poverty and inequality. His mother's addiction highlighted the devastating impact of the opioid epidemic, while his grandparents' struggles with alcohol and domestic violence mirrored the broader cultural challenges facing many Appalachian families.

Through these stories, he made the case that the personal and the systemic are deeply intertwined. Addiction, poverty, and instability were the result of cultural and economic forces that had been building for generations. By grounding his critique in his own experiences, Vance gave readers a tangible connection to the abstract problems facing rural America.

While Vance's personal narrative was steeped in empathy, his broader analysis didn't shy away from uncomfortable truths. He critiqued cultural norms that, in his view, perpetuated cycles of poverty and despair. These included a sense of fatalism that discouraged ambition, a reliance on government assistance without a focus on self-improvement, and a distrust of institutions that could provide support.

Vance didn't make these critiques lightly. He understood the pain and frustration that led to these behaviors, having witnessed them firsthand. But he also believed that cultural change was essential to breaking the cycle of poverty. This tension—between understanding and critique—was central to *Hillbilly Elegy*, making it both a deeply empathetic and unflinchingly honest account.

While much of Vance's analysis focused on cultural factors, he also addressed systemic failures that had exacerbated the struggles of working-class Americans. He highlighted the inadequacies of public education in places like Middletown, where schools often lacked the resources to prepare students for higher education or skilled careers. He critiqued the healthcare system, which failed to adequately address the opioid epidemic and mental health crises ravaging communities. And he pointed to economic policies that had left industrial towns behind, contributing to the widespread sense of hopelessness that permeated regions like Appalachia. He wanted readers to see that the challenges facing his community were part of a larger pattern that required both cultural and institutional change.

One of the defining tensions in *Hillbilly Elegy* was Vance's effort to balance empathy for individuals with a critical lens on cultural behaviors and choices. He deeply loved and respected the people he wrote about, particularly his grandparents, who had been the bedrock of his survival. At the same time, he felt a responsibility to call out behaviors and attitudes that, in his view, perpetuated hardship.

This balancing act wasn't always easy. Vance knew his critiques might be controversial, particularly among those who felt he was placing too much emphasis on personal responsibility and not enough on systemic barriers. But for Vance, the two weren't mutually exclusive. He believed that addressing inequality required both structural reforms and cultural introspection—a perspective shaped by his own journey.

Above all, Vance was committed to authenticity. He didn't want *Hillbilly Elegy* to come across as an academic treatise or a detached analysis. By grounding the book in his personal experiences, he hoped to create something that felt real, relatable, and deeply human. It was this authenticity that made the book resonate with readers from all walks of life, sparking a national conversation about class, culture, and the future of the American Dream.

Writing *Hillbilly Elegy* was a deeply personal and emotionally taxing process for JD Vance. It required him to revisit some of the most difficult moments of his life, translate them into a narrative that resonated universally, and grapple with the knowledge that his family's struggles would become part of a public conversation. From outlining the book's themes to navigating the publishing world, Vance's journey as a first-time author was peppered with challenges, self-discovery, and an uncompromising belief in the importance of his story.

Vance wrote *Hillbilly Elegy* with a clear purpose: to share his personal experiences in a way that shed light on the challenges facing working-class Americans. He started by outlining the book's structure, identifying key themes such as resilience, the impact of family, and the systemic forces that perpetuated poverty and addiction. Each theme was anchored in anecdotes from his own life, from his tumultuous childhood in Middletown to his transformative years in the Marines and at Yale.

Organizing these stories into a coherent narrative was no small task. Vance struggled to decide how much of his personal life to include and how to connect his experiences to broader cultural and economic issues. He wanted the book to resonate with readers who had never set foot in Appalachia, while also honoring the authenticity of his community's struggles. Striking this balance required careful thought and constant revisions.

Much of the early writing process involved gathering memories and stories that encapsulated the book's themes. Vance revisited pivotal moments from his childhood—his mother's battle with addiction, Mamaw's tough love, and Papaw's quiet strength—while also reflecting on the larger cultural forces at play. He supplemented these memories with insights from his time in the Marines and at Yale, drawing connections between his personal journey and the systemic challenges he had observed.

Writing *Hillbilly Elegy* meant exposing his family's most vulnerable moments to public scrutiny, a decision Vance did not take lightly. He often wrestled with guilt and self-doubt, wondering if sharing these stories would be seen as betrayal or exploitation. His mother's addiction, in particular, was a deeply painful subject. While Vance believed that including it was essential to understanding the book's message, he also knew it would reopen old wounds for both himself and his family.

Conversations with his relatives, particularly about how they would be portrayed, were often difficult. Vance sought to ensure that the book reflected their humanity and resilience, even as it acknowledged their flaws. Mamaw's memory loomed especially large during the writing process. Her influence, both as a stabilizing force and as a symbol of Appalachian grit, shaped much of the book's tone and message. Vance often thought about how she would have reacted to the memoir, drawing strength from the knowledge that she had always encouraged him to tell the truth, no matter how hard it was.

Revisiting his past was an emotional ordeal. Writing about moments of fear, anger, and loss brought back memories Vance had worked hard to suppress. There were times when the process felt overwhelming, as though he were reliving the chaos and instability of his childhood. Yet, Vance also found catharsis in the act of writing. By confronting these memories head-on, he gained a deeper understanding of himself and the forces that had shaped his life.

One of the biggest challenges was finding a writing style that felt authentic and accessible. He wanted *Hillbilly Elegy* to provide a cultural critique that resonated with readers from all walks of life. Using his deeply personal stories as an access point, he blended recollections with broader reflections on poverty, class, and opportunity, all while maintaining a tone that was engaging and relatable.

Drawing on lessons from his Yale mentors and professional experiences, Vance crafted a voice that was conversational yet insightful, unflinching yet empathetic. He avoided academic jargon and instead wrote in a way that felt grounded and approachable, ensuring that his message could reach as wide an audience as possible.

Vance's time at Yale played a significant role in shaping his approach to writing. Professors who had encouraged him to embrace his unique perspective as a strength inspired him to tell his story with honesty and nuance. His exposure to public policy debates and legal frameworks also informed his analysis, helping him connect personal anecdotes to larger systemic issues.

Like many first-time authors, Vance faced rejection when he first began pitching *Hillbilly Elegy* to publishers. Some questioned whether there was an audience for his story, while others expressed doubt about its marketability. These rejections were demoralizing, and Vance often worried that his story wouldn't resonate beyond the Appalachian and working-class communities it described.

Despite these setbacks, Vance remained committed to his vision. He believed deeply in the importance of sharing his story and its potential to spark meaningful conversations about class, culture, and opportunity. With the encouragement of friends, mentors, and early readers who saw the value in his work, Vance pushed forward, refining his manuscript and seeking out publishers who understood his message.

Eventually, his perseverance paid off. When *Hillbilly Elegy* was picked up for publication by Harper Press, it was both a validation of Vance's hard work and a reminder of the barriers he had overcome to get there.

The process of writing *Hillbilly Elegy* was a journey of self-reflection, resilience, and determination. Vance poured his heart into the book, blending personal vulnerability with cultural critique to create a narrative that was both deeply personal and universally resonant. While the road to publication was not without its challenges, his commitment to sharing his story ultimately paid off, setting the stage for the book's remarkable impact.

*   *   *

When *Hillbilly Elegy* hit bookshelves in 2016, it quickly became a sensation. Vance's deeply personal account of his upbringing resonated across cultural and political divides, sparking debates that went far beyond his own story. The book's raw honesty and cultural relevance earned it widespread acclaim, but it also provoked intense criticism and controversy. As *Hillbilly Elegy* became a centerpiece in discussions about the white working class—particularly in the context of Donald Trump's 2016 presidential victory—it cemented Vance as a prominent, albeit polarizing, voice in American literature and public discourse.

Upon its release, *Hillbilly Elegy* received glowing reviews from major publications. Outlets like *The New York Times*, *The Wall Street Journal*, and *The Washington Post* praised the memoir for its unflinching portrayal of life in Appalachia and its insight into the cultural and economic struggles of working-class Americans. Critics lauded Vance's ability to weave personal anecdotes with broader cultural observations, creating a narrative that was both intimate and universally resonant.

Many reviewers noted the book's timeliness, with *The Atlantic* calling it "a powerful window into a misunderstood demographic" and *The Economist* describing it as "essential reading for anyone trying to understand the social fractures of modern America." Vance was celebrated as a fresh and compelling voice in American literature, someone who could speak with authority on issues that had long been overlooked by mainstream media.

What set *Hillbilly Elegy* apart for many readers was its raw honesty. Vance's willingness to confront painful memories and critique cultural norms in his community was seen as both brave and necessary. His nuanced perspective—simultaneously empathetic and critical—gave the book a depth that resonated with readers across the political spectrum. For many, *Hillbilly Elegy* offered a much-needed glimpse into the realities of rural and working-class life, challenging stereotypes and sparking conversations about resilience, identity, and opportunity.

While *Hillbilly Elegy* was widely praised, it also became the subject of heated debates. For some, the book was an eye-opening account of the struggles facing rural America, shedding light on issues like addiction, economic decline, and cultural isolation. These readers saw Vance's story as a testament to the resilience of the human spirit and a call to action for policymakers and communities to address systemic challenges.

However, others criticized the book for what they perceived as oversimplifications and sweeping generalizations. Some felt that Vance's emphasis on personal responsibility overshadowed the systemic forces driving poverty and inequality, while others argued that his critiques of Appalachian culture were overly harsh and lacked nuance. These debates often reflected broader tensions in American society, as discussions about *Hillbilly Elegy* became proxies for debates about class, race, and political identity.

Among the book's most vocal critics were people from Appalachia itself. Some felt that *Hillbilly Elegy* painted an unfairly negative picture of the region, focusing too heavily on dysfunction and failing to capture its richness and diversity. Appalachian writers and activists argued that Vance's narrative, while valid, was just one perspective and shouldn't be taken as representative of the entire region.

Others accused Vance of perpetuating harmful stereotypes, particularly about poor white communities. They argued that his critiques of cultural norms—such as fatalism, addiction, and dependence on government assistance—were reductive and ignored the systemic challenges that had shaped those behaviors. While Vance's defenders saw his critiques as a necessary part of the conversation, his detractors worried that the book reinforced negative perceptions of Appalachia without offering meaningful solutions.

In academic and political circles, *Hillbilly Elegy* sparked robust discussions about its conclusions and implications. Sociologists, economists, and political scientists debated the book's portrayal of class and culture, with some praising its insights and others questioning its methodology and framing. Politicians on both sides of the aisle referenced the book in discussions about rural policy, though often with vastly different interpretations of its message.

For Vance, these debates underscored the complexity of the issues he had written about. While he welcomed the conversations sparked by *Hillbilly Elegy*, he also acknowledged the limitations of his perspective, often reminding readers that his story was just one piece of a much larger puzzle.

The release of *Hillbilly Elegy* coincided with a seismic shift in American politics. Donald Trump's 2016 presidential campaign, fueled by populist rhetoric and promises to revitalize struggling communities, brought the struggles of the white working class into the national spotlight. Vance's memoir, with its focus on the very demographic that had helped propel Trump to victory, became a key text for those seeking to understand the political and cultural forces at play.

Journalists, pundits, and policymakers often referenced *Hillbilly Elegy* in discussions about the "forgotten Americans" who felt left behind by globalization and cultural change. The book's nuanced portrayal of working-class struggles provided a counterpoint to simplistic narratives, helping to illuminate the deeper forces driving political and social discontent.

Beyond the media, *Hillbilly Elegy* also had a significant impact on policymakers and scholars. The book's exploration of addiction, economic decline, and cultural disconnection informed discussions about public policy, particularly in areas like healthcare, education, and economic development. For some, Vance's story highlighted the urgent need for systemic change; for others, it underscored the importance of fostering personal responsibility and resilience within communities.

The reception of *Hillbilly Elegy* was as complex and multifaceted as the issues it addressed. While it earned Vance widespread acclaim and a national platform, it also sparked debates about representation, responsibility, and the intersection of personal narrative and cultural critique. For better or worse, the book became a defining text of its time, shaping conversations about class, identity, and the future of rural America.

The release of *Hillbilly Elegy* catapulted Vance into the national spotlight, transforming him from a first-time author into a public intellectual, thought leader, and, for many, a symbol of the struggles facing rural and working-class America. The book's success opened doors to media platforms, professional opportunities, and, eventually, the political stage. However, the recognition also came with significant pressure, as Vance found himself navigating the complexities of representing a demographic while staying true to his personal beliefs.

*   *   *

When *Hillbilly Elegy* became a bestseller, Vance quickly emerged as a leading voice on issues of class, poverty, and cultural disconnection. The memoir's raw honesty and relevance to the political moment made Vance a sought-after commentator, with media outlets eager to hear his insights on the forces shaping rural America. Appearances on major platforms like *The New York Times*, *NPR*, and *Meet the Press* introduced him to a wide audience, establishing him as a public intellectual with a seat at the national conversation.

Vance's media presence was marked by his ability to communicate complex issues in a way that was both relatable and thought-provoking. Whether discussing the opioid crisis, economic decline, or the cultural divide between urban and rural America, Vance brought a nuanced perspective that resonated with viewers across ideological lines. His authenticity and willingness to confront difficult topics made him a compelling figure in an era of political and cultural polarization.

Beyond media appearances, Vance was invited to speak at universities, think tanks, and conferences, where he addressed audiences ranging from academics to policymakers. These speaking engagements allowed him to expand on the themes of *Hillbilly Elegy*, exploring the systemic and cultural challenges facing working-class communities and proposing solutions rooted in both personal responsibility and structural reform.

As a speaker, Vance's appeal lay in his ability to bridge divides. He could connect with rural audiences who saw their struggles reflected in his story, while also engaging with elites who sought to better understand the forces driving discontent in regions like Appalachia. This dual role as both a storyteller and an analyst solidified his reputation as a thought leader and set the stage for his future endeavors.

As *Hillbilly Elegy* gained traction, Vance found himself positioned as a spokesperson for rural and working-class Americans. While he had always intended to shed light on the challenges facing his community, the extent to which he became a symbol surprised even him.

Journalists, policymakers, and readers looked to Vance not only for his insights but also as a representative of a demographic that had long been underrepresented in national conversations.

This role came with both opportunities and challenges. On one hand, it allowed Vance to elevate the voices of working-class Americans, bringing attention to issues like addiction, economic stagnation, and cultural disconnection. On the other hand, it placed a heavy burden on him to balance his personal beliefs with the expectations of those who saw him as their advocate.

Being a symbol for an entire demographic was a double-edged sword. Vance was acutely aware that his story, while representative in some ways, was not universal. He faced criticism from those who felt that *Hillbilly Elegy* oversimplified or misrepresented the complexities of Appalachian life. At the same time, he struggled with the pressure to align his public statements with the expectations of those who identified with his story.

Vance approached this tension by staying true to his values and focusing on the issues he felt were most important. While he couldn't represent every facet of working-class America, he could use his platform to spark conversations and advocate for meaningful change. This balance—between being a voice for his community and an independent thinker—defined his public persona in the years following *Hillbilly Elegy*'s release.

The success of *Hillbilly Elegy* opened doors that might have otherwise remained closed. Vance's newfound prominence led to opportunities in venture capital, where he joined a firm focused on investing in businesses that could drive economic growth in underserved communities. This role allowed him to apply his insights into systemic challenges in a practical way, exploring how private investment could address some of the issues he had highlighted in his book.

Vance also became increasingly involved in public service, participating in initiatives aimed at addressing the opioid crisis and promoting economic development in rural areas. These experiences deepened his understanding of policy and governance, preparing him for the eventual decision to enter the political arena.

While Vance had not initially envisioned a career in politics, the reception of *Hillbilly Elegy* and the opportunities it created began to shift his perspective. The book's success demonstrated the power of storytelling in shaping public discourse, and he saw how his platform could be used to influence policy and advocate for the communities he cared about. Over time, the idea of running for office became less of a distant possibility and more of a tangible goal.

The themes of *Hillbilly Elegy*—resilience, opportunity, and the importance of bridging divides—would become central to Vance's political philosophy. His ability to connect with both rural voters and urban elites positioned him as a unique figure in American politics, one who could navigate the complexities of a polarized nation while staying grounded in his own story.

Hillbilly Elegy did more than introduce Vance to the world—it transformed him into a national figure, a thought leader, and a symbol of rural America's struggles and aspirations. The book's success opened doors to media platforms, professional opportunities, and, eventually, the political stage. While the recognition came with challenges, Vance embraced his role, using his platform to advocate for change.

*   *   *

Years after the release of *Hillbilly Elegy*, Vance has had time to reflect on the impact of the memoir that catapulted him to national prominence. For him, the book was always intended as a tool for sparking meaningful conversations about class, opportunity, and the forces shaping rural and working-class America. While the reception of the book has been both rewarding and complex, *Hillbilly Elegy* remains a cultural touchstone, its legacy intertwined with the ongoing debates about the American Dream and the challenges facing communities like Middletown.

Looking back, Vance often expresses gratitude for the opportunity to share his story with the world. Writing *Hillbilly Elegy* was a deeply personal process, one that forced him to confront painful memories and reflect on the forces that shaped his life. The book's success affirmed the value of that vulnerability, showing Vance that his story resonated with people from all walks of life.

Vance has often spoken about how readers have reached out to share their own experiences, thanking him for putting words to struggles they had felt but never fully articulated. These moments of connection have been some of the most rewarding aspects of the book's legacy, reminding Vance that his story is part of a larger tapestry of resilience and hope.

At the same time, Vance acknowledges the challenges that came with exposing his life to public scrutiny. Writing openly about his family's struggles—particularly his mother's addiction and his grandparents' volatile marriage—was not an easy decision, and the backlash from some quarters was difficult to navigate. Critics from within Appalachia, as well as those outside the region, sometimes accused Vance of perpetuating stereotypes or simplifying complex issues.

Vance has reflected on these criticisms with a mix of humility and resolve. While he acknowledges that *Hillbilly Elegy* represents his perspective rather than a comprehensive account of Appalachian life, he stands by the importance of telling his truth. For Vance, the memoir's purpose was not to define an entire region but to spark a conversation about the challenges facing working-class Americans—and in that sense, he believes it succeeded.

Since its release, *Hillbilly Elegy* has become a cornerstone in discussions about class, opportunity, and the American Dream. Its exploration of themes like addiction, economic decline, and cultural disconnection has resonated far beyond Appalachia, offering insights into the struggles faced by working-class communities across the country.

Policymakers, academics, and journalists have continued to reference the book in their analyses of rural America and the broader challenges of inequality. Whether praised or critiqued, *Hillbilly Elegy* has played a central role in shaping how these issues are understood and discussed, cementing its place as a cultural artifact of a pivotal moment in modern American history.

Hillbilly Elegy is often seen as a reflection of the cultural and political climate of the mid-2010s, particularly in the wake of Donald Trump's 2016 presidential victory. The book's focus on the white working class and its disconnection from elite institutions resonated in a moment of deep polarization and social upheaval. As such, it has been studied not just as a memoir but as a lens through which to understand the forces driving political and cultural change in America.

Vance recognizes that the book's relevance has evolved over time. While it was initially seen as a commentary on a specific demographic and moment, its themes of resilience, opportunity, and cultural critique have continued to resonate in new and unexpected ways. For Vance, this enduring relevance is both a testament to the universality of the story and a reminder of the work that remains to be done.

As Vance continues to channel the lessons of the book into his work in public service, business, and politics, one thing is certain: the memoir may have been his first major contribution to the national dialogue, but it was only the beginning of his efforts to create a more equitable and hopeful future for all Americans. And he would do that through politics.

"Public service must be more than doing a job efficiently and honestly. It must be a complete dedication to the people and to the nation."
— Margaret Chase Smith

Entering the Political Arena

When *Hillbilly Elegy* turned JD Vance into a household name, his life changed in ways he never could have anticipated. As a bestselling author and a rising figure in venture capital, Vance found himself uniquely positioned to influence the national conversation about the challenges facing rural and working-class Americans. Yet, for all his public visibility, Vance initially resisted the idea of stepping into the political spotlight. The prospect of public scrutiny, the toll on his family, and the polarized political landscape gave him pause.

But as the years passed and the issues he cared about deepened— economic inequality, the opioid epidemic, and a widening cultural divide— Vance began to see politics as a natural extension of his advocacy. Encouraged by family, mentors, and political allies, Vance began to weigh the risks and rewards of running for office, ultimately deciding that the opportunity to make a tangible impact was worth the challenges ahead.

By the time Vance began to seriously consider a political career, *Hillbilly Elegy* had already cemented his place in the national spotlight.

The book's success had given him a platform to speak about the issues he cared most about—poverty, addiction, and the struggles of working-class communities. Through media appearances, speaking engagements, and discussions with policymakers, Vance had become a trusted voice on these topics, but he often felt that the conversations stopped short of meaningful action.

Vance's work in venture capital further shaped his understanding of the challenges facing rural America. As a partner at a firm focused on investing in businesses that could revitalize struggling communities, he saw firsthand the systemic barriers that stifled economic growth in places like Middletown. These experiences deepened his resolve to address inequality and fueled his desire to take on a more active role in shaping policy.

Despite his growing visibility, Vance was reluctant to enter the political arena. The idea of running for office came with significant personal and professional risks. He knew that stepping into the public eye would invite intense scrutiny—not just of his policies and positions but of his personal life and family.

He also grappled with the reality of the polarized political landscape. The toxic nature of modern politics, with its constant attacks and tribalism, seemed far removed from the meaningful conversations he wanted to have. For him, the question wasn't just whether he could win—it was whether he could make a difference in a system that often prioritized soundbites over solutions.

Ultimately, it was Vance's deep concern for the struggles of the working class that pushed him toward politics. The issues he had written about in *Hillbilly Elegy*—economic stagnation, addiction, and cultural disconnection—had only grown more urgent in the years since the book's release. In Ohio, the opioid epidemic continued to devastate families, while the decline of manufacturing and other industries left many communities without a clear path forward.

Vance believed that his unique perspective, shaped by both his personal experiences and his professional work, positioned him to address these challenges in ways that traditional politicians could not. He saw an opportunity to bring a fresh voice to the table, one that understood the struggles of working-class Americans not from a distance but from firsthand experience.

The decision to run for office wasn't one Vance made lightly. He spent months discussing the idea with family, friends, and trusted mentors, weighing the potential risks and rewards. His wife, Usha, was a central figure in these conversations, offering both unconditional support and a clear-eyed assessment of the challenges they would face as a family.

Vance also sought advice from political allies and mentors, many of whom encouraged him to step into the arena. They saw his story as a powerful asset, one that could resonate with voters and bring much-needed authenticity to modern politics. While Vance remained cautious, these conversations helped him see the potential impact he could have as a candidate and, ultimately, as a leader.

The transition from author to politician was a step Vance took with hesitation but also with conviction, driven by a deep desire to address the issues he had spent years writing and speaking about. As he prepared to launch his campaign, he knew that the road ahead would be challenging, but he was ready to bring his unique voice and perspective to the political stage. He would run for Senate.

*　　　*　　　*

JD Vance's Senate campaign was rooted in a clear mission: to speak directly to the concerns of working-class Ohioans who felt left behind by both political parties. Drawing from his personal story and the themes of *Hillbilly Elegy*, Vance crafted a campaign that resonated with the struggles and aspirations of everyday voters. While he faced challenges from rivals and skeptics, his ability to connect with Ohioans on a personal level became a defining feature of his campaign.

Vance's campaign centered on a set of issues that were deeply relevant to Ohio's working-class communities. Economic growth and job creation were top priorities, particularly in regions hit hardest by the decline of manufacturing. Vance emphasized the need to bring back industries, invest in infrastructure, and create opportunities for skilled laborers.

The opioid crisis, a deeply personal issue for Vance, was another key focus. He spoke openly about the devastating impact addiction had on his family and pledged to support policies that would address the crisis comprehensively, from improving access to treatment to holding pharmaceutical companies accountable.

He also made revitalizing rural communities a cornerstone of his campaign. He argued that the cultural and economic disconnection between rural America and urban centers was not just a social issue but a national one, advocating for investments in education, healthcare, and broadband infrastructure to bridge the gap.

At the heart of Vance's message was his personal story—a narrative that many voters found relatable and inspiring. He often spoke about his upbringing in Middletown, the influence of his grandparents, and his journey from a struggling household to Yale Law School. This story of resilience and determination allowed Vance to connect with voters on an emotional level, framing himself not as a career politician but as someone who understood their struggles firsthand.

Vance's authenticity was a key part of his appeal. He didn't shy away from discussing his family's challenges or the mistakes he had made along the way, instead using these experiences to underscore his commitment to advocating for those who felt abandoned by the system.

Vance's ability to connect with voters was evident on the campaign trail, where he made a point of engaging directly with Ohioans in their communities. From town halls to factory visits, he prioritized face-to-face interactions, listening to the concerns of constituents and sharing his vision for the future.

At one town hall in a struggling industrial town, Vance spoke about the need to rebuild the middle class by investing in local businesses and supporting workforce development programs. His remarks were met with nods of agreement and personal stories from attendees about their own struggles to make ends meet. These moments of connection revealed his ability to bridge the gap between policy discussions and real-world impact.

Vance's visits to factories and small businesses also highlighted his commitment to understanding the needs of Ohio's workforce. He spent time talking with workers about the challenges they faced, from stagnant wages to unsafe working conditions, and incorporated their feedback into his campaign proposals. These interactions reinforced his message that his campaign was about serving the people, not special interests or party politics.

Using an approach to campaigning that was rooted in listening, he recognized that the best way to address voters' concerns was to understand them fully. Therefore, he made a concerted effort to adapt his strategies based on the feedback he received.

For example, after hearing from rural voters about the lack of healthcare access in their communities, Vance doubled down on his commitment to expanding healthcare infrastructure in underserved areas. Similarly, his conversations with small business owners informed his proposals to reduce regulatory burdens and create a more supportive environment for entrepreneurship.

Vance's campaign was not without its challenges. Within the Republican Party, he faced criticism from rivals who questioned his conservative credentials and labeled him an opportunist. Some pointed to his past criticisms of Donald Trump as evidence that he was out of step with the party's base, forcing Vance to address these concerns head-on.

He countered these attacks by emphasizing his alignment with conservative values and his commitment to policies that prioritized working-class Americans. His endorsement by Donald Trump ultimately helped solidify his support among the Republican base, giving his campaign a significant boost.

On the other side of the aisle, Democrats targeted Vance's lack of political experience and his connections to Silicon Valley, painting him as out of touch with the realities of Ohio's working class. They also criticized his book, *Hillbilly Elegy*, arguing that it perpetuated stereotypes about Appalachia and oversimplified complex issues.

Vance responded to these criticisms by staying focused on his campaign message. He acknowledged his outsider status but framed it as a strength, arguing that his lack of political experience gave him a fresh perspective and a willingness to challenge the status quo. He also used his book as a platform to discuss the systemic challenges facing rural America, highlighting his commitment to addressing these issues through concrete policy proposals.

Perhaps the biggest challenge JD faced was overcoming skepticism about his credibility as a first-time candidate. Many voters were unsure whether he could transition from the world of writing and venture capital to the demands of public office. To address these doubts, JD focused on demonstrating his understanding of policy and his ability to deliver results.

Through detailed policy proposals, thoughtful debate performances, and consistent messaging, Vance worked to establish himself as a serious candidate with a clear vision for Ohio's future. His willingness to engage with voters and address their concerns directly helped build trust and credibility over the course of the campaign.

Overall, Vance's Senate campaign was defined by his ability to connect with working-class voters and craft a message that spoke directly to their needs. By leveraging his personal story, focusing on key issues, and engaging with voters on the ground, he built a campaign that resonated deeply with Ohioans.

In a competitive Senate race that demanded not only policy expertise but also political credibility, endorsements played a pivotal role in Vance's campaign. Among them, the backing of former President Donald Trump stood out, as it energized the Republican base and positioned Vance as a frontrunner. Coupled with support from other influential figures and organizations, these endorsements helped Vance overcome initial skepticism and establish himself as a serious contender. However, navigating the benefits and challenges of such high-profile support required careful strategy, as Vance worked to balance his alignment with Trump's populist platform while maintaining his own distinct voice.

Receiving Donald Trump's endorsement was a defining moment in JD Vance's campaign, instantly elevating his visibility and solidifying his standing with Republican voters. In a state like Ohio, where Trump's populist message had resonated strongly in both the 2016 and 2020 elections, the former president's backing was a signal to voters that Vance was a trusted ally. The endorsement helped energize the Republican base, bringing enthusiasm and momentum to a campaign that was still fighting to gain traction.

Vance's own personal populist messaging, which focused on revitalizing working-class communities, combating corporate overreach, and addressing cultural divides, aligned closely with Trump's own platform. This alignment made the endorsement feel authentic to voters who saw Vance as someone capable of continuing Trump's legacy while bringing his unique perspective to the table.

Securing Trump's endorsement was no small feat. Behind the scenes, Vance's campaign worked diligently to demonstrate that he was the candidate best suited to carry forward the former president's vision for America. This involved direct communication with Trump's team, strategic positioning on key issues, and a careful effort to address concerns about Vance's past criticisms of Trump during the 2016 election.

Ultimately, it was Vance's personal story, his focus on the struggles of working-class Americans, and his ability to connect with voters that won Trump over. Trump's public endorsement, delivered at a rally in Ohio, was a moment of validation for Vance's campaign, drawing significant media attention and galvanizing support among Republican voters.

The impact of Trump's endorsement was immediate and far-reaching. It brought national attention to Vance's campaign, increasing his media coverage and raising his profile within the Republican Party. The endorsement also bolstered his fundraising efforts, attracting contributions from donors who viewed him as a viable candidate with the potential to win. Perhaps most importantly, it gave him credibility among conservative voters who had been skeptical of his commitment to their values.

While Trump's endorsement was the most high-profile, Vance also garnered support from other influential figures and organizations within the conservative movement. High-profile Republicans, including senators and governors, lent their voices to his campaign, vouching for his character and policy platform. These endorsements helped Vance appeal to different factions within the Republican Party, broadening his base of support.

Additionally, endorsements from conservative advocacy groups and think tanks provided JD's campaign with valuable resources, from policy expertise to grassroots mobilization. Organizations focused on issues like economic development, opioid addiction, and rural revitalization saw Vance as a candidate who could bring attention to their causes and advance their agendas.

The combination of high-profile endorsements and grassroots support was critical to Vance's success. Local leaders, community organizations, and volunteers rallied behind his campaign, helping to amplify his message across Ohio. These endorsements translated into tangible support in the form of campaign events, voter outreach, and fundraising efforts.

By building a coalition of supporters at both the national and local levels, Vance was able to create a campaign that felt both credible and connected to the communities he sought to represent.

But while Trump's endorsement was a major asset, it also came with challenges. Vance had to navigate the fine line between aligning with Trump's populist platform and maintaining his own voice and policy focus. This required careful messaging, particularly on issues where Vance's views diverged slightly from Trump's or where he wanted to emphasize his own priorities.

Vance's campaign leaned heavily into shared themes, such as standing up for the working class, challenging the influence of elites, and revitalizing American manufacturing. At the same time, he worked to distinguish himself by highlighting his personal experiences and his vision for addressing Ohio-specific challenges, such as the opioid epidemic and rural infrastructure needs.

One of Vance's key strategies was to remain authentic in his messaging. While he welcomed Trump's endorsement and embraced the support of the Republican base, he was careful not to let his campaign be defined solely by the former president. Vance framed his alignment with Trump as part of a broader commitment to the principles that resonated with voters—economic opportunity, cultural renewal, and strong leadership—rather than as blind loyalty to any one figure.

This approach allowed Vance to appeal to a wide range of voters, from staunch Trump supporters to independents who were drawn to his personal story and pragmatic solutions. By balancing his alignment with Trump's platform with his own unique voice, Vance was able to maintain credibility while staying true to his vision for Ohio.

*   *   *

The final stretch of JD Vance's Senate campaign was a whirlwind of events, debates, and strategic outreach. As polls tightened and the race drew national attention, Vance's team worked tirelessly to shore up support among the Republican base while appealing to undecided and independent voters.

One of the campaign's pivotal moments came during a televised debate where Vance faced off against his Democratic opponent. Vance's performance merged policy expertise and personal authenticity, as he deftly defended his platform while emphasizing his working-class roots. He spoke passionately about issues like the opioid crisis, rural revitalization, and the importance of bringing manufacturing jobs back to Ohio. While his opponent sought to paint him as inexperienced and out of touch, Vance countered with a narrative that connected with voters: he wasn't a career politician but someone who understood Ohio's struggles because he had lived them.

High-profile events in the campaign's final weeks, including rallies with prominent Republican figures like Donald Trump, further galvanized his supporters. These events drew large crowds and media attention, showcasing Vance's ability to energize voters and position himself as a key figure in the Republican Party's future.

A key focus of Vance's campaign in its final weeks was persuading undecided voters, particularly in swing districts and suburban areas. Vance's strategy centered on emphasizing his authenticity and his commitment to addressing Ohio's most pressing challenges. He highlighted his personal experiences with addiction and poverty, framing them as evidence of his deep understanding of the issues facing many Ohioans.

His campaign also doubled down on local outreach, organizing town halls, door-to-door canvassing, and targeted advertising that addressed the specific concerns of different communities. By tailoring his message to resonate with voters' unique needs, Vance was able to build a coalition that spanned rural, suburban, and urban areas.

As the race heated up, Vance faced a barrage of attacks from his opponents, who questioned his political experience, criticized his connections to Silicon Valley, and challenged his commitment to Ohio. Vance's campaign responded by emphasizing his deep roots in the state and his track record of advocating for working-class Americans.

Vance's ability to stay on message and maintain a calm, confident demeanor in the face of these attacks helped reinforce his credibility with voters. He framed the criticisms as distractions from the real issues, positioning himself as the candidate focused on solutions rather than partisan mudslinging.

*   *   *

Election night was a culmination of months of hard work, and the atmosphere at Vance's campaign headquarters was a mix of nervous anticipation and cautious optimism. Surrounded by family, friends, and campaign staff, Vance watched as the results began to trickle in. Early returns showed a tight race, with both candidates trading leads as votes were counted in key districts.

As the night progressed, the tide began to turn in Vance's favor. Strong turnout in rural and suburban areas, coupled with his ability to make inroads in traditionally Democratic strongholds, gave him a decisive edge. By the time the race was called in his favor, the mood at campaign headquarters had shifted from tense anticipation to unbridled celebration.

When the final results were announced, JD's reaction was one of quiet gratitude and reflection. He took a moment to absorb the significance of the victory. For someone who had grown up in a struggling household in Middletown, the journey to the U.S. Senate was a testament to resilience, determination, and the belief in the possibility of change.

Usha, a constant source of support throughout the campaign, was visibly emotional, while their children, too young to fully grasp the moment's importance, basked in the excitement of the celebration. Vance's campaign staff, many of whom had been with him from the beginning, cheered as the reality of the win set in.

Vance's victory was a defining moment for Ohio and the broader Republican Party. For Ohioans, the win signaled a renewed focus on the struggles of the working class and a commitment to addressing the state's most pressing issues. Vance's campaign had successfully tapped into the frustrations and hopes of voters who felt overlooked by traditional politics, offering a vision of economic renewal and cultural restoration.

For the Republican Party, Vance's win represented the rise of a new generation of conservative leaders. His combination of populist messaging, policy pragmatism, and personal authenticity made him a standout figure within the party, signaling a potential shift in its approach to addressing the concerns of rural and working-class Americans. The culmination of Vance's efforts and the belief of his supporters had come to fruition in a victory that was as much about Ohio's future as it was about his own.

*   *   *

From his first day in office, JD Vance made it clear that his legislative agenda would center on the issues most pressing to Ohioans. The opioid crisis, a deeply personal issue for Vance, was at the top of his list. He pushed for bipartisan measures to expand access to addiction treatment, strengthen community health programs, and hold pharmaceutical companies accountable for their role in the epidemic. Vance's proposals included increased funding for rural healthcare centers and initiatives to combat the stigma surrounding addiction.

Economic revitalization was another cornerstone of Vance's early work. He introduced legislation aimed at incentivizing investment in manufacturing and infrastructure projects, particularly in areas hit hardest by industrial decline. Vance emphasized the need for federal support in rebuilding local economies, advocating for tax breaks for small businesses and funding for workforce development programs.

Rural development was a natural extension of these efforts. Vance championed policies to expand broadband access, improve public schools, and address infrastructure challenges in Ohio's rural communities. His goal was to bridge the gap between rural and urban areas, ensuring that all Ohioans had access to the resources they needed to thrive.

As a freshman Senator, Vance faced the challenge of learning the ropes in a complex and often contentious political environment. While his outsider status had been an asset during his campaign, it also meant that he had to quickly adapt to the rules and norms of the Senate. Vance approached this task with the same determination that had defined his campaign, seeking out mentors and allies who could guide him through the legislative process.

Vance's ability to communicate effectively and connect with people served him well in this new role. Whether negotiating with colleagues on legislation or advocating for Ohio's needs in committee hearings, Vance's authenticity and focus on solutions helped him build relationships and earn respect on both sides of the aisle.

One of Vance's key challenges as a Senator was balancing his conservative principles with the need for bipartisan collaboration. While he remained committed to his campaign promises, Vance recognized that achieving meaningful progress often required working with colleagues who held different views.

Navigating the realities of political compromise wasn't always easy. There were moments when he had to weigh the potential benefits of a bill against the concessions it required, and he faced criticism from both sides for his decisions. However, Vance remained focused on the bigger picture, emphasizing that his ultimate goal was to improve the lives of Ohioans.

Vance often reflected on the lessons he had learned from his own life: that resilience and pragmatism were essential to overcoming challenges. This perspective guided his approach to leadership, allowing him to stay true to his values while navigating the complexities of governance.

Throughout his time in the Senate, Vance made it a priority to stay connected with the people of Ohio. He frequently returned to his home state to hold town halls, visit businesses and schools, and meet with constituents. These visits allowed Vance to hear directly from Ohioans about their concerns and priorities, ensuring that his work in Washington remained grounded in the needs of his community.

Whether speaking with factory workers about job creation or meeting with healthcare providers to discuss the opioid crisis, Vance's interactions with constituents reinforced his commitment to serving as a voice for the people who had elected him.

Vance's work in the Senate reflected the promises he had made during his campaign. From introducing legislation to support rural development to advocating for policies that addressed addiction and economic inequality, Vance's focus remained on the issues that mattered most to Ohioans.

*   *   *

The transition from private citizen to public servant was both challenging and transformative for Vance. On the campaign trail, he had learned to communicate with diverse audiences, articulate his vision under pressure, and navigate the intense scrutiny that came with running for office. As a Senator, these lessons deepened. Vance discovered the complexities of policymaking, the necessity of building coalitions, and the importance of listening—not just to constituents, but also to colleagues with differing viewpoints.

Vance often reflected on how his personal experiences shaped his approach to leadership. The values instilled in him by his grandparents—resilience, grit, and loyalty—served as guiding principles in his work. Whether drafting legislation or debating policies, Vance drew on the lessons of his past to ground himself in authenticity and purpose.

One of the greatest challenges Vance faced was balancing the demands of his political career with his responsibilities as a husband and father. The pressures of public life, from constant travel to relentless scrutiny, often made it difficult to find time for his family. Yet, Vance remained committed to ensuring that his role as a father and husband never took a backseat to his political ambitions.

Vance often credited his wife, Usha, as his anchor during this transition. Her constant support and practical wisdom helped him navigate the highs and lows of public life. Together, they worked to create a sense of normalcy for their children, even as Vance's career brought them into the spotlight.

This balancing act wasn't without its struggles, but it reinforced Vance's belief in the importance of staying grounded. By prioritizing his family and maintaining a strong connection to his roots, JD was able to navigate the challenges of public life with humility and focus.

The lessons he learned, both on the campaign trail and in the Senate, shaped him into a leader capable of succeeding in modern politics while remaining deeply connected to his roots. As he looked ahead, Vance saw the opportunity to leave a lasting impact on the nation.

At the same time, political analysts began identifying JD as a rising star within the GOP, pointing to his ability to energize voters, craft thoughtful policy, and engage with diverse constituencies. His increasing visibility on national platforms, from interviews to high-profile events, reinforced his image as a forward-looking leader who could help shape the party's future.

"If you want to go fast, go alone. If you want to go far, go together."
— African Proverb

Running Mate for Trump

T he 2024 election cycle began as one of the most contentious and closely watched in modern American history. The nation, already deeply polarized, faced growing economic uncertainties, cultural tensions, and debates over the future of democracy itself. Against this backdrop, former President Donald Trump announced his decision to run for a second non-consecutive term, setting the stage for another highly charged presidential campaign. As speculation swirled about who Trump would select as his running mate, the announcement of JD Vance—a political newcomer but rising Republican star—sent shockwaves through the political world.

According to CBS News, Vance had flown to Mar a Lago on July 13 and met with Trump. Later that day, Trump survived an attempted assassination in Pennsylvania at a rally in Butler. Two days later, on July 15, the first day of the Republican National Convention, Vance received a call from Trump asking him to be his running mate.

Twenty minutes later, Trump hopped on Truth Social and said, "After lengthy deliberation and thought, and considering the tremendous talents of many others, I have decided that the person best suited to assume the position of Vice President of the United States is Senator J.D. Vance of the Great State of Ohio."[4]

Vance was loyal from the start. On Day 3 of the Republican National Convention, Vance gave a speech. He told attendees, "The only thing that we need to do right now, the most important thing that we can do for those people, for that American nation that we all love, is to re-elect Donald J Trump president of the United States," Vance said.[5]

He continued, "Mr. President, I will never take for granted the trust you have put in me and what an honor it is to help achieve the extraordinary vision that you have for this country. Now, I pledge to every American, no matter your party, I will give you everything I have to serve you and to make this country a place where every dream you have for yourself, your family and your country will be possible once again."

*   *   *

By 2024, America's political landscape had become defined by deep divisions. Economic concerns, including inflation and stagnant wages, dominated headlines, while debates over immigration, climate policy,

---

[4] Alison Main and Eric Bradner, "Trump Selected Ohio Sen. JD Vance, a Critic Turned Ally, as Running Mate after Last-Minute Push from Son | CNN Politics," CNN, July 16, 2024, https://edition.cnn.com/2024/07/15/politics/trump-vp-pick-jd-vance/index.html.

[5] "JD Vance Tells Republican Convention 'people Who Govern This Country Have Failed and Failed Again' – as It Happened." The Guardian, July 18, 2024. https://www.theguardian.com/us-news/live/2024/jul/17/rnc-jd-vance-speech-trump-day-3-live-updates.

and cultural identity continued to polarize the electorate. Rural and working-class voters, in particular, felt increasingly alienated by what they saw as a political system disconnected from their struggles.

Donald Trump's re-entry into the presidential race further underscored the high stakes of the election. For his supporters, Trump represented a chance to "finish the job" he had started during his first term, while his critics viewed his candidacy as a dire threat to democratic norms. Amid this intense political climate, the choice of a running mate took on heightened importance, as voters and analysts speculated about who could best complement Trump's platform and appeal to key constituencies.

Trump's selection process for a running mate was shrouded in secrecy, fueling widespread speculation. Would he choose a political veteran to balance his ticket or a fresh face to energize his base? Names floated by pundits included sitting governors, prominent senators, and conservative media personalities. Vance's inclusion in these conversations initially surprised some observers, given his relative inexperience on the national stage. However, his personal story, populist appeal, and alignment with Trump's vision made him an increasingly compelling choice.

The announcement immediately dominated news cycles. Supporters of the Trump-Vance ticket hailed the choice as a masterstroke, praising Vance's ability to connect with rural and working-class voters. Conservative commentators lauded the decision as a sign that Trump's campaign was serious about addressing the concerns of Middle America.

However, the announcement was not without controversy. Critics questioned Vance's lack of national political experience, arguing that his rapid rise to prominence left unanswered questions about his preparedness for such a critical role. Others viewed his selection as an attempt to double down on Trump's populist appeal rather than broaden the ticket's base.

On social media, reactions ranged from enthusiastic endorsements to sharp critiques. For every voter inspired by Vance's story, there was another skeptical of his qualifications or concerned about the ticket's broader implications for the nation.

For Vance himself, the moment was both exhilarating and humbling. In interviews following the announcement, he spoke candidly about his decision to join the ticket. He acknowledged the weight of the responsibility he had taken on. Becoming Trump's running mate meant stepping into one of the most scrutinized and high-pressure roles in American politics. While he expressed confidence in his ability to rise to the occasion, he was clear-eyed about the challenges ahead, describing the campaign as a battle for the soul of the country.

The announcement of JD Vance as Donald Trump's running mate signaled that America could expect a campaign focused on amplifying the voices of rural and working-class Americans while doubling down on the populist themes that had defined Trump's political brand. For Vance, the role was both an opportunity and a test—a chance to advocate for the values he held dear while navigating the complexities of a national campaign.

The decision to choose Vance as Donald Trump's running mate in the 2024 presidential campaign was not made in isolation. It was the culmination of Vance's rapid ascent in the Republican Party and his growing reputation as a voice for working-class Americans. Behind the scenes, Trump's team considered various contenders for the role, but Vance's authenticity, populist appeal, and strategic advantages ultimately made him the ideal choice. For both Trump and Vance, the partnership symbolized a campaign focused on economic revival, cultural conservatism, and a return to national strength.

Of course, Vance's tenure as a Senator was instrumental in solidifying his place as a rising star within the Republican Party. His focus on working-class issues, from tackling the opioid epidemic to revitalizing rural economies, earned him widespread recognition and respect. His ability to speak authentically about the struggles of Middle America resonated not only with voters but also with Republican leaders who saw him as a fresh, relatable figure capable of energizing the party's base.

During his time in the Senate, Vance established himself as a policy-focused leader who could bridge the gap between traditional conservatives and the party's growing populist wing. His efforts to advocate for economic fairness, stand up to corporate overreach, and address systemic inequalities highlighted his commitment to serving as a voice for the voiceless—qualities that aligned closely with Trump's political brand.

Vance's appeal extended across critical voter demographics, making him a valuable asset for the Republican Party. In rural areas, his personal story of overcoming adversity resonated deeply, while his focus on job creation and community revitalization struck a chord with suburban voters. His ability to communicate effectively with these groups positioned him as a unifying figure who could bring together diverse constituencies under the Republican banner.

This demographic reach was particularly significant in swing states like Ohio, where his popularity and influence could help tip the balance in a closely contested election. For Trump, selecting Vance as his running mate was a way to solidify support in these key regions while reinforcing the campaign's commitment to addressing the concerns of everyday Americans.

*   *   *

Behind the scenes, the search for Trump's running mate was marked by intense speculation, with several high-profile figures floated as potential candidates: Senator Tim Scott, Governor Kristy Noem, former governor Nikki Haley, Representative Marjorie Taylor Greene, and others were named as significant possibilities. Other governors, senators, and even prominent media personalities like entrepreneur Vivek Ramaswamy were considered, each bringing their own strengths to the table. Some contenders were seen as safe choices, offering experience and stability, while others represented bold, unconventional picks aimed at shaking up the race.

For Vance, the prospect of being chosen was both exciting and daunting. While his name had been mentioned in media circles, he was aware of the stiff competition and the high stakes involved. Privately, Vance maintained his focus on his Senate duties, letting his track record speak for itself.

Ultimately, Trump's decision to choose Vance was rooted in several key factors. The two shared a populist message centered on economic revival, cultural renewal, and a rejection of establishment politics. Vance relatability and his ability to articulate the struggles of working-class Americans aligned perfectly with Trump's campaign vision.

Trump's team also recognized the strategic value of Vance's appeal in swing states like Ohio, which had been pivotal in Trump's previous electoral victories. Vance's presence on the ticket offered the potential to energize rural and suburban voters, build momentum in key battlegrounds, and reinforce the campaign's connection to its core base. In private discussions, Trump reportedly expressed admiration for Vance's authenticity and ability to connect with voters on a personal level.

Vance's selection as running mate was a calculated move designed to complement Trump's campaign strategy. While Trump's appeal to his base remained strong, Vance brought a fresh perspective and an ability to reach voters who might have been skeptical of Trump's combative style. Together, they represented a ticket that balanced experience with innovation, combining Trump's established brand with Vance's rising influence.

The campaign's core themes—economic revival, cultural conservatism, and national strength—were reinforced by Vance's presence on the ticket. His focus on addressing the opioid crisis, revitalizing rural communities, and standing up to corporate elites mirrored Trump's messaging, creating a cohesive narrative that resonated with voters.

Vance's selection also carried significant symbolic weight. As someone who had risen from a tumultuous upbringing to become a U.S. Senator and bestselling author, Vance embodied the American Dream that the campaign sought to champion. His story reinforced the ticket's promise to restore hope and opportunity to struggling communities, making him a relatable and inspiring figure for millions of Americans.

*   *   *

JD Vance's greatest political asset was his ability to connect with voters who felt ignored or betrayed by the political establishment.

Growing up in Middletown, Ohio, and witnessing firsthand the decline of manufacturing, the rise of the opioid epidemic, and the struggles of working-class families, Vance spoke with authenticity and empathy about issues that many politicians only addressed in talking points.

For voters in rural and post-industrial America, Vance's story was their story. He wasn't just someone who understood their challenges—he had lived them. This relatability made him an effective messenger for Trump's campaign, which sought to position itself as a champion for the "forgotten Americans." Vance's speeches often highlighted themes of resilience, community, and the promise of economic renewal, resonating with audiences across ideological lines.

While Vance was firmly aligned with the Republican Party, his message also struck a chord with independents and disaffected Democrats who felt alienated by both parties. His focus on working-class issues, cultural values, and practical solutions transcended partisan divides, making him an appealing figure for voters seeking authenticity and common ground. This cross-party appeal added a layer of versatility to the Trump-Vance ticket, helping it reach voters who might have otherwise been reluctant to engage with the Republican platform.

Vance's political philosophy and policy priorities aligned closely with Donald Trump's America First agenda. Both leaders emphasized the need to prioritize American jobs, secure energy independence, and strengthen the country's borders. Vance's focus on combating the opioid crisis—a deeply personal issue for him—further reinforced the ticket's commitment to addressing issues that directly impacted working-class families.

On the campaign trail, Vance's speeches often echoed Trump's themes while adding his own voice and perspective. For example, while Trump highlighted the importance of deregulation and trade reform, Vance often framed these issues through the lens of their impact on families and communities. This ability to amplify Trump's message while making it deeply personal enhanced the ticket's overall appeal.

Vance's rise to prominence as a bestselling author and Senator brought a level of intellectual depth and relatability that added credibility to the campaign. His ability to articulate complex issues in plain language, combined with his lived experience of poverty and resilience, gave the Trump-Vance ticket a unique dynamic. Vance's presence on the ticket signaled a commitment to addressing the root causes of economic and social discontent, lending the campaign an air of seriousness and purpose that extended beyond partisan rhetoric.

Furthermore, Vance's Ohio roots were a significant factor in his selection as Trump's running mate. Ohio had long been a bellwether state in presidential elections, and Vance's popularity in the state made him a valuable asset for the campaign. His ability to energize voters in both rural and suburban areas of Ohio was critical to securing the state's electoral votes and building momentum in neighboring swing states like Pennsylvania and Michigan.

Beyond Ohio, Vance's story and message resonated with voters in other key battleground states that shared similar economic and cultural challenges. His presence on the ticket helped the campaign solidify its appeal in regions that had been pivotal to Trump's victories in 2016.

Vance also brought a generational advantage to the Trump-Vance ticket. As a younger leader, he had the ability to connect with millennial and Gen Z voters who were often skeptical of establishment politicians. His authenticity, combined with his focus on issues like affordable healthcare, education reform, and economic opportunity, allowed him to engage with younger conservatives in a way that felt relevant and inspiring.

But Vance's appeal to these voters wasn't just about age—it was about the way he framed his message. He spoke to the anxieties and aspirations of a new generation, offering a vision of conservatism that was both grounded in traditional values and forward-looking in its solutions.

As Trump's running mate, Vance embraced the dual challenge of supporting the broader campaign message while emphasizing his own policy expertise and vision. During rallies and appearances, Vance often played the role of a measured counterbalance to Trump's fiery rhetoric. While Trump's speeches galvanized crowds with sweeping declarations of "Making America Great Again," Vance focused on the details—breaking down how policies would directly impact working-class families.

Vance's ability to pivot between Trump's big-picture messaging and his own nuanced discussions of policy allowed the ticket to appeal to a wide range of voters. For die-hard Trump supporters, Vance's alignment with the campaign's populist themes reinforced their enthusiasm. For more skeptical voters, Vance's intellectual depth and relatable demeanor provided reassurance about the ticket's credibility.

The dynamic between Trump and JD on the campaign trail was a study in contrasts that worked to the ticket's advantage. Trump, the seasoned showman, commanded attention with his larger-than-life presence and signature bluntness. Vance, by contrast, brought a quieter but equally compelling energy, offering thoughtful commentary and personal anecdotes that connected with voters on an emotional level.

Their joint appearances often felt like a well-rehearsed act, with Trump delivering the red-meat lines that fired up the base and Vance stepping in to elaborate on the practicalities of the campaign's policies. This balance allowed the two to complement each other, creating a dynamic that felt both engaging and strategic.

Vance played an active role in shaping the campaign's policy platform, particularly on issues where his expertise and personal experience were most relevant. His input on addressing the opioid crisis went beyond rhetoric, incorporating evidence-based strategies for expanding treatment programs, funding community healthcare, and holding pharmaceutical companies accountable.

Vance also pushed for policies aimed at revitalizing the middle class, including tax incentives for small businesses, investments in workforce development, and initiatives to rebuild infrastructure in rural communities. His contributions gave the campaign a more grounded and detailed policy framework, complementing Trump's broader themes of economic revival and national strength.

One of Vance's strengths was his ability to present complex policies in a way that felt accessible and relatable to voters. Whether discussing national security, healthcare, or education reform, Vance often framed his arguments through personal anecdotes or stories from constituents he had met on the trail. This approach made policy discussions feel less abstract and more connected to the everyday lives of voters.

Vance's authenticity was a hallmark of his campaign trail appearances. At town halls, factory visits, and small community gatherings, he listened intently to voters' concerns and responded with empathy and candor. Unlike many politicians, Vance often avoided scripted responses, opting instead for honest dialogue that reflected his own experiences and convictions.

Vance's ability to connect with voters was particularly evident in the personal stories he shared and the moments of genuine connection he fostered. At a campaign stop in West Virginia, a mother approached Vance to talk about her son's struggle with addiction. Instead of offering platitudes, Vance shared his own family's story and promised to continue fighting for better resources and support.

Beyond mere photo opportunities, these interactions were a reflection of Vance's commitment to staying grounded and engaged with the people he sought to serve. For many voters, these moments were a powerful reminder of why they believed in the Trump-Vance ticket.

*   *   *

The Trump-Vance ticket generated a wide spectrum of reactions from voters, political commentators, and the media. While many celebrated the pairing as a bold and strategic move that blended populist appeal with fresh leadership, others viewed it with skepticism or outright criticism. JD Vance's working-class roots and compelling personal story bolstered the ticket's appeal in critical swing states, but his alignment with Donald Trump invited sharp scrutiny from opponents and some factions within the Republican Party. The public perception of the ticket reflected the broader polarization of the 2024 election, with reactions ranging from enthusiastic support to fierce opposition.

For Donald Trump's core supporters, the addition of Vance to the ticket was seen as an inspired choice. Vance's populist message, grounded in his own experiences of overcoming adversity, resonated deeply with voters who felt disillusioned with establishment politics. His focus on issues like economic revival, the opioid crisis, and rural development reinforced the campaign's commitment to addressing the concerns of working-class Americans.

Trump's base also appreciated Vance's authenticity. Unlike career politicians, Vance's rise from a struggling family to a seat in the U.S. Senate felt relatable and genuine. At rallies and campaign events, supporters frequently commented on how Vance "spoke their language" and understood the challenges they faced.

Vance's selection as running mate was particularly well-received in swing states like Ohio, Pennsylvania, and Michigan, where his Midwestern roots and focus on manufacturing jobs resonated with key voting blocs. Voters in these states, many of whom had felt alienated by both major parties, saw Vance as a credible advocate for their concerns.

In suburban areas, Vance's measured demeanor and policy expertise helped bridge the gap with moderate Republicans and independents who were wary of Trump's more confrontational style. His ability to appeal to these critical demographics gave the ticket an edge in regions that would prove decisive in the election.

On the other side of the aisle, Democratic opponents wasted no time in critiquing Vance's record and his alignment with Trump. They portrayed Vance as a political opportunist, pointing to his previous criticisms of Trump during the 2016 election and framing his embrace of Trump's platform as an act of convenience rather than conviction.

Vance's lack of extensive national political experience was another frequent target. Critics argued that his relatively short tenure in the Senate left him ill-prepared for the demands of the vice presidency, let alone a role in shaping national policy during a turbulent time.

While Vance enjoyed widespread support from Trump's base, not all Republicans were convinced. Some members of the party's establishment wing questioned the choice of a running mate with limited experience and a profile closely tied to Trump's populist movement. These critics worried that the ticket's focus on populist rhetoric might alienate traditional conservatives and undermine efforts to broaden the party's appeal.

Despite these challenges, Vance remained steadfast in his messaging, emphasizing his commitment to the issues that mattered most to voters. His ability to navigate criticism with poise and focus helped mitigate some of the skepticism, though doubts lingered among certain factions of the party.

Major media outlets took notice of Vance's rapid rise within the Republican Party, often framing him as a symbol of its populist evolution. Profiles of Vance highlighted his compelling backstory, his success as an author, and his ability to connect with voters in key demographics. Conservative-leaning media celebrated Vance as a fresh and authentic voice who could carry Trump's message while appealing to a broader audience.

Vance's thoughtful approach to policy discussions, particularly on issues like the opioid crisis and rural development, also garnered praise from political analysts who saw him as a serious and credible addition to the ticket.

At the same time, Vance faced sharp criticism from progressive media, which questioned his qualifications and scrutinized his positions on cultural and economic issues. Some outlets painted him as an enabler of Trump's divisive rhetoric, arguing that his alignment with the former president undermined his claims of bridging divides and advocating for the working class.

JD's past comments and writings, particularly those in *Hillbilly Elegy*, were re-examined in the context of the campaign, with critics accusing him of perpetuating stereotypes about Appalachia and oversimplifying complex societal issues. These narratives added to the intensity of media coverage, making Vance a polarizing figure in the public eye.

Throughout the campaign, Vance demonstrated a knack for handling media scrutiny with a blend of humility and confidence. In interviews, he addressed criticisms head-on, often redirecting the conversation back to the core issues of the campaign.

Vance's willingness to engage with tough questions, combined with his ability to articulate a clear vision for the country, helped him maintain credibility even in the face of relentless scrutiny. His authenticity and focus on substance resonated with voters who were tired of political grandstanding, further solidifying his appeal.

The public perception of the Trump-Vance ticket reflected the broader polarization of American politics in 2024. For supporters, JD Vance represented a fresh, authentic voice who could bring credibility and relatability to the campaign's populist message. For critics, he was a controversial figure whose alignment with Trump raised questions about his vision for the country.

*   *   *

The Trump-Vance ticket shook things up in the Republican Party itself, reshaping its identity, priorities, and appeal heading into the 2024 election and beyond. JD Vance's selection as Donald Trump's running mate brought new energy to the party's base, while also broadening its demographic reach and influencing its policy focus. At the same time, the ticket faced the challenge of uniting the GOP's diverse factions, with Vance playing a pivotal role in bridging divides and shaping the party's vision for the future.

The inclusion of Vance invigorated the Republican Party's core supporters, particularly in rural and working-class communities. His personal story, which mirrored the struggles of many voters in these areas, made him a relatable and authentic figure who could articulate their frustrations and aspirations. By emphasizing issues like job creation, the opioid crisis, and cultural renewal, Vance reinforced the party's commitment to addressing the concerns of everyday Americans.

At rallies and campaign events, Vance's speeches often struck an emotional chord with audiences, blending policy details with personal anecdotes that resonated deeply. His ability to connect with voters on a human level helped solidify support for the ticket and energized volunteers, donors, and grassroots organizers across the country.

Vance's presence on the ticket also helped the Republican Party reach beyond its traditional base. His focus on working-class issues, combined with his Midwestern roots, appealed to disillusioned voters who had felt ignored by both major parties. In swing states like Ohio, Pennsylvania, and Michigan, Vance's relatability and focus on economic renewal attracted independent voters and former Democrats who were drawn to the ticket's populist message.

Vance's appeal wasn't limited to rural areas. In suburban districts, his measured tone and policy expertise reassured moderates and younger conservatives who were skeptical of Trump's more polarizing rhetoric. This ability to connect with a diverse range of voters helped the GOP expand its coalition and gain traction in key battleground regions.

Vance's policy focus significantly influenced the Republican platform for the 2024 election. His emphasis on addressing the opioid epidemic, revitalizing manufacturing, and investing in rural infrastructure became central themes of the campaign. These priorities reflected Vance's belief in the importance of tangible solutions to the economic and social challenges facing Middle America.

By integrating Vance's ideas into the party's broader agenda, the GOP signaled a shift toward a more populist and community-focused vision. This approach resonated with voters who were eager for leadership that prioritized their needs over partisan politics or corporate interests.

Vance's selection as Trump's running mate also marked the beginning of his long-term influence within the Republican Party. As a younger leader with a compelling personal story and a clear policy vision, Vance was widely seen as a key figure in the party's future. Political analysts speculated that his role on the ticket could pave the way for greater leadership opportunities, positioning him as a potential presidential candidate in the years to come.

Vance's ability to combine populist themes with thoughtful policy discussions set him apart from many of his peers, earning him respect from both the party's grassroots supporters and its intellectual circles. His rise within the GOP signaled a potential evolution of the party's identity, one that prioritized working-class concerns while maintaining its commitment to conservative principles.

One of the key challenges for the Trump-Vance ticket was uniting the Republican Party's diverse factions. While Trump's influence over the party remained strong, divisions between traditional conservatives, libertarians, and populists created tensions that needed to be addressed. Vance's role as a bridge between these groups was critical to the campaign's success.

Vance's ability to connect with both grassroots supporters and establishment figures helped ease concerns about the ticket's direction. By emphasizing shared goals—such as economic growth, national security, and cultural renewal—Vance worked to unite the party under a common vision. His thoughtful approach to policy discussions also reassured skeptics who were wary of Trump's more polarizing rhetoric.

Despite these efforts, the Trump-Vance ticket faced challenges from within the GOP. Some establishment Republicans were critical of the ticket's populist direction, fearing that it might alienate suburban voters and business interests. Others questioned Vance's readiness for the national stage, citing his relative inexperience in politics.

Vance addressed these criticisms head-on, using his campaign appearances and media interviews to emphasize his qualifications and his commitment to serving the American people. His focus on unity and his willingness to engage in open dialogue with skeptics helped mitigate some of the internal tensions, allowing the campaign to maintain momentum.

*　　　*　　　*

For Vance, serving as a vice-presidential candidate was both an honor and a trial by fire. The relentless pace of the campaign, coupled with the intense media scrutiny and the weight of representing millions of voters, tested his stamina and resolve. Yet, Vance embraced these challenges, using them as opportunities for growth.

In interviews following the campaign, Vance reflected on the defining moments that shaped his experience. From addressing hostile questions during debates to engaging directly with voters on the campaign trail, Vance spoke about the importance of authenticity and empathy in building trust and connecting with people, listening, and working to make their lives better.

The campaign also deepened Vance's understanding of the issues that mattered most to voters and refined his approach to leadership. Hearing directly from constituents across the country reinforced his belief in the need for policies that prioritize working-class Americans, strengthen communities, and restore economic opportunity. Vance's experience on the national stage also highlighted the importance of bridging divides—not just between political parties, but within communities. "

As a vice-presidential candidate, Vance's public image evolved significantly. Once primarily known as the author of *Hillbilly Elegy* and a Senator from Ohio, Vance emerged from the campaign as a national figure—a voice for rural and working-class America with a unique ability to articulate the struggles and aspirations of these communities. While the campaign brought criticism and controversy, it also solidified Vance's reputation as a thoughtful, relatable, and determined leader.

*   *   *

The Trump-Vance ticket left an indelible mark on the Republican Party, signaling a continued shift toward populist themes and a focus on the concerns of Middle America. Vance's emphasis on issues like the opioid crisis, rural development, and economic revitalization helped broaden the party's appeal, particularly in regions and demographics that had traditionally felt alienated by national politics.

Political analysts speculated that Vance's role in the campaign would influence the party's platform for years to come, with younger leaders looking to him as a model for combining populist messaging with thoughtful policy proposals. Whether the Republican Party would fully embrace this vision remained an open question, but Vance's presence in the campaign undoubtedly reshaped the party's trajectory.

The Trump-Vance ticket also had significant cultural and political implications beyond the Republican Party. By centering the struggles of working-class Americans in their messaging, the campaign brought renewed attention to issues that had long been overlooked in national discourse. Topics like addiction, job creation, and rural infrastructure became focal points of the election, forcing candidates from both parties to address these concerns more substantively.

However, the ticket's success also sparked intense debates about the role of populism in American politics. Supporters praised the campaign for giving a voice to forgotten communities and challenging the status quo, while critics raised concerns about the divisive rhetoric and policy priorities that accompanied it. Vance's role as a measured and relatable counterpart to Trump added nuance to these discussions, highlighting the potential for populism to be both empathetic and solutions-driven.

As the campaign came to a close, speculation about Vance's political future reached a fever pitch. Many viewed his performance as a vice presidential candidate as a stepping stone to greater leadership roles, with some even suggesting that he could be a frontrunner for the presidency in future elections. Vance, for his part, remained focused on the immediate task of serving the American people.

The 2024 campaign tested Vance's resilience, refined his vision, and elevated his profile on the national stage. The experience left him with a deeper understanding of the challenges facing America and a renewed commitment to addressing them with integrity and compassion.

The legacy of the Trump-Vance ticket, meanwhile, extended far beyond the campaign trail. By shining a spotlight on the struggles of working-class and rural Americans, the ticket reshaped the political conversation and set the stage for a new era of Republican leadership. Whether this legacy would endure, and how it would evolve, remained to be seen—but one thing was certain: JD Vance had emerged as a key figure in the future of American politics.

"We must adjust to changing times and still hold to unchanging principles."
— Jimmy Carter

Leading America into 2025 as Vice President

On that brisk January morning inside the Rotunda of the Capitol Building, JD Vance raised his right hand, flanked by his family and the newly re-elected President Donald Trump, and made history.

Vance's ascension to the vice presidency carried immense historical weight, particularly for the communities he represented. As the first vice president from Appalachia, Vance symbolized the resilience and determination of a region often overlooked in national politics. For working-class Americans, his rise was a testament to the possibility of change—a reminder that someone who shared their struggles and understood their challenges could reach the highest echelons of power.

For Middletown and communities like it, Vance's vice presidency offered a sense of validation. Residents saw in him a reflection of their own aspirations, a leader who would bring their concerns to the forefront of national discussions. Local leaders and community members spoke with pride about the significance of his journey, instilling a strong sense of hope for future generations.

Vance's unique background as the child of a struggling family in a declining industrial town added a layer of cultural symbolism to his role. Unlike many of his predecessors, Vance's path to the vice presidency was not paved by privilege or political dynasties but by resilience and ambition. His story resonated across partisan lines, offering a narrative of perseverance that transcended ideological divides.

This cultural symbolism extended beyond Appalachia. Vance's life story served as a powerful reminder that the American Dream—though battered—was still alive, and that leadership could emerge from unexpected places. His presence in the White House challenged stereotypes about who could lead and what it meant to represent the nation.

For the nation, JD's ascension to the vice presidency marked a moment of possibility—a chance to bridge divides, uplift forgotten communities, and forge a path toward a more inclusive and resilient future.

*   *   *

As Vance begins his tenure as the fiftieth vice president of the United States, the nation watches with anticipation and curiosity. His inauguration marked the start of a new chapter not only for his own remarkable journey but also for the communities he has vowed to represent. With his immense personal experience, policy expertise, and a fresh perspective on leadership, Vance has entered office poised to tackle some of the most pressing challenges facing the country.

Vance's vice presidency promises to bring renewed focus to the concerns of working-class Americans, particularly those in rural and industrial communities who have long felt left behind. Drawing from his own experiences growing up in Middletown, Vance has consistently emphasized the importance of restoring the American Dream for families struggling to make ends meet. He's considered the "poster child" for Project 2025, the conservative blueprint for reshaping the United States encapsulated in a 900-page document, *Mandate for Leadership*, published by conservative thinktank the Heritage Foundation.

His administration's early priorities are expected to include revitalizing manufacturing and tackling the opioid crisis.

Vance has expressed a commitment to supporting policies that bring jobs back to American soil, particularly in regions hit hardest by industrial decline. His focus on workforce development and economic incentives for domestic production could pave the way for a new era of American manufacturing.

With the opioid epidemic continuing to devastate communities across the nation, Vance is likely to lead efforts to expand treatment options, hold pharmaceutical companies accountable, and invest in preventive measures. His personal connection to this issue suggests a vice president deeply invested in finding tangible solutions. Already, the strategy of implementing tariffs on Canada, Mexico, and China, countries from which fentanyl is flowing over the borders into the United States, is poised to make an impact.

Beyond these areas, one of Vance's defining traits has been his ability to connect with a wide range of audiences, from blue-collar workers to suburban moderates. As vice president, he is uniquely positioned to act as a bridge between the administration and Congress, fostering bipartisan cooperation on key issues like infrastructure, healthcare, and rural development.

Vance's measured and pragmatic approach offers hope for progress on issues that transcend partisan divides. His emphasis on finding common ground could help reduce the gridlock that has plagued Washington in recent years, creating opportunities for meaningful reform.

As vice president, Vance is expected to bring a fresh perspective to the role, redefining what it means to serve as the nation's second-in-command. While the vice presidency is often seen as largely ceremonial, Vance has made it clear that he intends to be an active and engaged leader, working closely with President Trump to implement their shared vision for America.

Vance skillfully leverages his ability to forge a personal connection to policy. His speeches and initiatives often draw from his own life experiences, making policy feel relatable and grounded in real-world concerns.

Furthermore, while he shares Trump's populist appeal, Vance's approach is more detail-oriented, offering voters a deeper understanding of how policies will impact their lives.

JD Vance's vice presidency arrives at a critical moment for the nation. With economic disparities, cultural divisions, and global challenges demanding urgent attention, his role as a leader will be both demanding and transformative. His tenure has the potential to shape the future of the Republican Party, bringing a focus on working-class concerns and pragmatic policymaking that could redefine conservatism for a new generation.

Looking ahead, Vance's ability to balance his personal vision with the broader goals of the administration will be key. His leadership style, rooted in authenticity and resilience, offers a sense of hope that the vice presidency can be a platform for real change—one that bridges divides, uplifts communities, and restores faith in the American Dream.

As the nation moves forward through 2025 and beyond, all eyes will be on JD Vance, watching how he navigates the complexities of his new role and fulfills the promises of his historic tenure. While the challenges are immense, so too are the opportunities for leadership and progress.

"The strength of a nation derives from the integrity of the home."
— Confucius

JD Vance's Personal Life

For JD Vance, public service has always been deeply intertwined with the personal values and experiences that shaped him. While the demands of political leadership have thrust him into the spotlight, Vance has worked hard to preserve the private, grounded family life that serves as his anchor. Behind the speeches, policies, and campaign rallies lies a story of resilience, partnership, and a commitment to values that have guided him through life's challenges.

Navigating the pressures of being the vice president of the United States has only reinforced the importance of his personal foundation. In many ways, Vance's ability to remain connected to his roots and family life has been critical to his success in public office, offering him perspective and a source of strength in the face of immense responsibility.

At the heart of Vance's public life is a deep appreciation for the role his family has played in shaping his journey. From the unconditional love of his grandparents, Mamaw and Papaw, to the unwavering support of his wife, Usha, Vance's personal relationships have been a constant source of motivation and guidance.

Vance often credits his family with teaching him the values that now define his leadership style: resilience in the face of adversity, a relentless work ethic, and an unshakable commitment to the people and causes he believes in.

Maintaining a healthy work-life balance has been one of the most significant challenges of Vance's career in politics. The constant travel, public scrutiny, and demands of leadership often leave little room for personal time, yet Vance has made a conscious effort to prioritize his role as a husband and father.

In interviews, Vance has spoken candidly about the difficulty of carving out moments of normalcy amidst the whirlwind of political life. Whether it's reading bedtime stories to his children over the phone or finding quiet moments with Usha between campaign stops, Vance strives to ensure that his family remains a central part of his life, even during the busiest seasons.

Behind Vance's rise to national prominence is a story of partnership—one rooted in mutual respect, shared values, and a deep commitment to family. Vance's marriage to Usha Vance, a fellow Yale Law School graduate, has been a cornerstone of his personal and professional life. Their relationship, forged through a blend of intellectual connection and emotional support, has provided Vance with the stability and insight he has needed to navigate the complexities of public service. Together, Vance and Usha represent a partnership that transcends cultural and personal differences, creating a foundation for their family and shared vision for the future.

Vance and Usha's paths first crossed at Yale Law School, a place far removed from Vance's working-class roots in Middletown, Ohio. For Usha, a first-generation Indian-American raised in California, the elite academic environment was also a far cry from her parents' immigrant story. Despite their differing backgrounds, Vance and Usha were drawn to each other through their shared intellect, curiosity, and values.

In his memoir *Hillbilly Elegy*, Vance described Usha as one of the most brilliant people he had ever met, noting her sharp wit and compassionate nature. For her part, Usha admired Vance's resilience, work ethic, and his ability to approach life's challenges with both seriousness and humor. Their early conversations often touched on topics ranging from law and philosophy to the societal issues that Vance had experienced firsthand.

Vance and Usha's connection was grounded not only in shared intellectual interests but also in their mutual desire to understand and bridge cultural and socioeconomic divides. For Vance, Usha's perspective offered a window into a world of optimism and opportunity that complemented his own experiences of hardship and resilience. Usha, in turn, was inspired by Vance's determination to rise above his circumstances and make a difference in the lives of others.

As their relationship evolved, JD and Usha built a bond that was strengthened by their shared ambitions and mutual respect. After graduating from Yale, they supported each other through the early stages of their careers— Vance in venture capital and Usha as a law clerk for Supreme Court Chief Justice John Roberts.

Their backgrounds, though different, became a source of strength rather than division. Vance often spoke about how Usha's cultural heritage introduced him to new perspectives and traditions, while Usha embraced the values of loyalty, grit, and family that Vance carried from his Appalachian upbringing. Together, they found ways to navigate these contrasts, celebrating their differences while focusing on their common goals.

Vance and Usha have an admirable ability to blend two distinct cultural identities into a unified family life. Usha's Indian-American heritage brought elements of tradition, discipline, and celebration into their home, while Vance's Appalachian roots emphasized resilience, loyalty, and community. This cultural fusion has enriched their lives and taught them the value of adaptability and understanding—lessons they've carried into their parenting and public roles.

Throughout Vance's career, Usha has been a steadfast source of support and insight. As Vance grappled with the challenges of writing *Hillbilly Elegy*, running for Senate, and eventually stepping into the role of Vice President, Usha served as both a sounding board and an advisor. Her legal expertise and sharp analytical mind helped Vance navigate the complexities of political life, while her unwavering belief in his abilities bolstered his confidence during moments of doubt.

Vance often credits Usha with helping him maintain perspective, particularly during the most demanding periods of his career, keeping him grounded and focused.

Whether on the campaign trail, in the Senate, or stepping onto the national stage, Vance has drawn strength from his partnership with Usha. Her encouragement and guidance have been instrumental in shaping his vision for public service, reminding him of the values they both hold dear: integrity, compassion, and a commitment to creating opportunities for others.

As parents of three young children—two boys and a girl—Vance and Usha strive to create a home environment that reflects their shared values. They emphasize the importance of hard work, empathy, and education, instilling in their children a sense of responsibility and gratitude. Despite the demands of public life, Vance makes it a priority to spend quality time with his children, whether it's helping with homework, attending school events, or simply enjoying family dinners.

Vance often speaks about how his children provide a sense of grounding amidst the chaos of public life. Their innocence and curiosity remind him of the bigger picture, reinforcing his commitment to building a better future for the next generation.

As a family, the Vances have built a life that reflects their values and aspirations, serving as a powerful example of what can be achieved through mutual respect, understanding, and love. Together, they have worked to ensure that family remains at the heart of JD's life, even amidst the relentless pace of his career.

The high-stakes world of political leadership is often unforgiving, with long hours, constant travel, and unrelenting public scrutiny. For Vance, these demands intensified during his Senate campaign, continued through his term in Congress, and reached new heights with his role as vice president. These pressures have tested his ability to maintain a healthy work-life balance, forcing him to make difficult decisions about how to allocate his time.

Vance has spoken candidly about the moments when professional obligations clashed with personal commitments, such as missing a school event or a family dinner due to last-minute campaign stops or late-night policy meetings. Despite his best efforts, the demands of public life sometimes temporarily overshadow his family responsibilities. During his Senate campaign, for example, JD endured a particularly grueling stretch of back-to-back events that left him with little time to check in with Usha or his children. It forced him to reevaluate his priorities and find ways to better integrate his roles as a leader and a father.

Vance and Usha have also made efforts to shield their children from the pressures of public life, striving to create a sense of normalcy despite the spotlight. From bedtime stories and weekend outings to simple family dinners, they have worked to ensure that their home remains a place of stability and comfort. Vance often emphasizes the importance of keeping his children grounded, teaching them to appreciate life's blessings while staying humble and connected to their roots.

As Vance's career has grown, Usha has played a crucial role in managing their household and ensuring that their family remains a priority. Her ability to juggle the demands of her own career with the responsibilities of parenting has been instrumental in maintaining a sense of balance. Vance frequently credits Usha with creating the stability that allows him to focus on his work without losing sight of what matters most.

Usha has also been a steadying influence for Vance, particularly during the most chaotic moments of his political career. Whether it's offering advice on a tough decision, reminding him to take a step back and breathe, or simply being there as a listening ear, Usha has been an anchor for Vance as he navigates the complexities of public life. Her ability to keep their family grounded and focused on their shared values has been a source of strength for Vance, helping him stay true to his mission and purpose. As she stood at his side on that fateful day in the Rotunda, looking on admiringly as he took his oath, she left onlookers in no doubt she will continue to do so throughout Vance's tenure as vice president.

Preston D. Munro

"Character, in the long run, is the decisive factor in the life of an individual and of nations alike." — Theodore Roosevelt

A Man of Values

Throughout his life and career, JD Vance has been guided by a set of deeply ingrained personal values shaped by his upbringing, life experiences, and faith. These values—resilience, loyalty, empathy, and morality—have informed his leadership style, his approach to policymaking, and his interactions with constituents. They are the foundation of his public service and a constant reminder of the lessons he learned growing up in Middletown, Ohio.

Vance's childhood in a struggling industrial town taught him the importance of resilience. Growing up amidst economic decline, addiction, and instability, he learned early on that success requires determination and the ability to adapt in the face of hardship. Resilience isn't just about surviving tough times, he knows; it's about finding the strength to move forward.

This belief has shaped his approach to challenges in politics, whether it's advocating for legislation in a polarized Congress or navigating the scrutiny of public life. Vance's ability to persevere, even in the face of criticism or setbacks, reflects the grit he developed during his formative years.

In his political career, Vance has championed policies aimed at giving others the tools to overcome adversity. For example, his efforts to expand job training programs and combat the opioid epidemic stem from his belief that systemic barriers can be addressed with practical, targeted solutions. By focusing on resilience—not just as an individual trait but as a goal for communities— Vance has worked to empower those who feel left behind.

For Vance, family has always been at the core of his worldview. From the steadfast support of his grandparents, Mamaw and Papaw, to the partnership he shares with his wife, Usha, family has been both a source of strength and a guiding principle. This commitment extends beyond his immediate household to his broader sense of responsibility toward the American family, which he views as the backbone of the nation.

Vance's loyalty to his family has occasionally required him to make difficult choices. He believes that leadership begins at home and that staying grounded in personal commitments makes him a more effective public servant.

Growing up in poverty and witnessing the devastating effects of addiction gave Vance a firsthand understanding of the struggles many Americans face. These experiences led him to develop a sense of empathy that has become a defining characteristic of his leadership. Vance often emphasizes the importance of listening to others and meeting them where they are, whether on the campaign trail or in policymaking discussions.

Vance's empathy is evident in the policies he champions, particularly those aimed at supporting struggling communities. His work on addressing the opioid crisis, for instance, is deeply personal, rooted in his desire to prevent other families from experiencing the pain his own endured. Similarly, his efforts to invest in rural infrastructure and expand access to healthcare reflect a commitment to uplifting those who have been marginalized or overlooked.

Faith has played a quiet but profound role in Vance's journey. While he has not always been vocal about his religious beliefs, he grew up in a casual evangelical Christian environment and converted to Catholicism in 2019. He often reflects on the ways his faith has shaped his values and decisions, including beliefs like banning pornography, advocating for the nuclear family, and more. For Vance, faith provides a moral framework that guides his approach to leadership and reminds him of his responsibility to serve others.

Vance's moral compass, underpinned by traditional Christian values, has shaped key decisions throughout his career, even when they were politically risky. Moments of moral courage have earned Vance both criticism and respect, solidifying his reputation as a leader who prioritizes principles over partisanship.

Faith permeates Vance's worldview. In a Fox News interview, Vance used what he referred to as "a very Christian concept" to explain his views on immigration.[6] "You love your family and then you love your neighbor, and then you love your community, and then you love your fellow citizens in your own country, and then after that, you can focus

---

[6] Sigal Samuel, "JD Vance Accidentally Directed Us to a Crucial Moral Question," Vox, February 6, 2025, https://www.vox.com/future-perfect/398460/jd-vance-ordo-amoris-order-love-christianity-catholic-charity.

[on] and prioritize the rest of the world. A lot of the far left has completely inverted that," he noted.

Invoking the idea of ordo amoris, or "rightly ordered love," he managed to spark a debate on a concept that resonates not only with Christians but that brings together secular Americans as well.

Vance's career and decisions are a testament to the values that have shaped him: resilience, loyalty, empathy, and faith. These principles are the very foundation of his approach to leadership and his vision for the country. He has built strong connections and relationships with prominent Catholic thinkers, integralists, postliberal scholars, and conservative intellectuals such as Kevin Roberts, Patrick Deneen, and Sohrab Ahmari, refining his thinking through discourse. By staying true to his values, Vance has sought to create meaningful change while remaining grounded in the lessons of his own journey.

As Vance continues to navigate the responsibilities of the vice presidency, these values will remain central to his work, shaping his decisions as a leader and inspiring his efforts to build a better future for all Americans.

For Vance, the road to public leadership has been paved by challenges, sacrifices, and moments of profound personal and professional growth. Navigating the intense scrutiny of public life while balancing family commitments has required resilience, introspection, and a constant re-evaluation of priorities. Through it all, Vance has grown into a grounded and thoughtful leader, shaped by his struggles and strengthened by the support of his loved ones.

Vance's challenges—both personal and professional—have been instrumental in shaping his leadership style. The lessons he has learned from navigating adversity have instilled in him a deep sense of empathy, resilience, and accountability. As vice president, he draws on these experiences to guide his decisions, emphasizing the importance of listening, adapting, and staying true to one's principles.

Through the ups and downs of his career, Vance has remained focused on his long-term goals: uplifting struggling communities, creating opportunities for working-class Americans, and building a stronger, more united nation. His personal growth, rooted in family values and a commitment to service, has strengthened his resolve to lead with integrity and purpose.

In the end, JD Vance's journey is a testament to the power of his values. The challenges he has faced have not only shaped his character but also deepened his commitment to serving the American people. Through these struggles, JD has grown into a leader who values empathy, prioritizes family, and remains focused on creating a better future for all.

Vance's journey is far from over, but his vision for the future is clear. He remains committed to keeping his family at the center of his life, instilling the values that have shaped him into the next generation. At the same time, he continues to work toward a political legacy that reflects his principles and serves the people who inspired his journey from Middletown to the national stage.

As Vance looks ahead, his focus on resilience, loyalty, and service promises to guide not only his career but also the example he sets for his family and the country. In the years to come, he hopes that his story—and the values it embodies—will serve as a reminder of the power of perseverance, the importance of staying true to one's roots, and the enduring potential of the American Dream.

Vance's journey is a testament to the power of perseverance, faith, and the enduring importance of family. As he continues to lead the nation, he carries with him the lessons learned from his upbringing, the support of his loved ones, and the conviction that leadership is most meaningful when it is rooted in service to others. For Vance, the heart behind the leadership is, and always will be, family and values.

"You have enemies? Good. That means you've stood up for something, sometime in your life." — Winston Churchill

Controversies and Criticism

Public life is often a double-edged sword, and JD Vance is no exception to this rule. As a bestselling author, U.S. Senator, and now vice president, Vance has consistently found himself at the center of national conversations—not all of them favorable. Whether it's the cultural debates sparked by *Hillbilly Elegy*, his alignment with Donald Trump, or his policy positions, Vance's public persona has drawn both admiration and pointed criticism.

His story—a meteoric rise from a troubled childhood in Middletown, Ohio, to the heights of American politics—has inspired millions. Yet, it has also invited scrutiny, with detractors questioning his motives, methods, and message. This duality of public life, where praise and criticism coexist, has been a defining feature of Vance's career.

Controversy, while challenging, has played a role in shaping Vance as a leader. Understanding how he has navigated criticism offers insights not only into his character but also into the broader political and cultural forces at play in contemporary America.

JD Vance's *Hillbilly Elegy* thrust him into the national spotlight, earning widespread acclaim for its raw, unflinching portrayal of the struggles facing Appalachia and working-class America. Yet, the memoir also became a lightning rod for criticism. Some praised Vance for shedding light on a largely ignored demographic, while others accused him of oversimplifying complex social and economic issues.

Critics from Appalachia, in particular, took issue with what they saw as a narrow and, at times, disparaging view of their culture. Vance's descriptions of personal struggles, family dysfunction, and cultural stagnation were seen by some as perpetuating negative stereotypes rather than offering constructive solutions. "He painted us as a lost cause," one critic wrote. "But there's so much more to Appalachia than the struggles he chose to highlight."

Vance has often defended his work as a personal story rather than a definitive account of Appalachia. Despite the criticism, *Hillbilly Elegy* cemented Vance's reputation as a voice for the working class, even as it exposed him to a broader cultural debate about representation and accountability.

Similarly, Vance's alignment with Donald Trump has been both a political asset and a point of contention. While his support for Trump's policies has solidified his standing among the Republican base, it has also drawn criticism from moderates and progressives who question his motives. Detractors have accused Vance of abandoning his previous critiques of Trump in favor of political expediency, pointing to a perceived shift in tone from his earlier years to his Senate campaign and vice presidency.

Vance's policy stances on issues like immigration, economic protectionism, and education reform have also sparked debate. Supporters applaud his commitment to addressing working-class concerns, while opponents argue that some of his positions lack nuance or fail to consider broader implications.

For instance, in February 2025, shortly after ascending to the vice presidency, he clashed with the U.S. Conference of Catholic Bishops, accusing them of resettling "illegal immigrants" for federal funding. Cardinal Timothy Dolan labeled Vance's remarks as "scurrilous" and "nasty." Vance justified his stance using the medieval Catholic concept "ordo amoris," suggesting a hierarchy of care that prioritizes citizens over immigrants, a view disputed by theologians.[7]

In a 2021 interview, Vance mocked Democratic figures such as Kamala Harris and Transportation Secretary Pete Buttigieg for being childless, labeling them as "miserable" and lacking a "direct stake" in the nation's well-being.[8] He suggested that childless individuals should be taxed at a higher rate, prompting criticism from various outlets. Vance later defended his statements as humor.

In the face of these critiques, Vance has leaned into his populist messaging, emphasizing his connection to working-class voters. This approach has allowed Vance to maintain his authenticity among supporters, even as his detractors continue to question his alignment with Trump's vision.

---

[7] Peter Smith, "A Short Honeymoon for Catholics in D.C. as Vice President Vance Clashes with Bishops on Migration," AP News, February 6, 2025, https://apnews.com/article/jd-vance-catholic-bishops-migration-94138954824b68dbd0b29b28504e056e.

[8] Gilles Paris, "US Presidential Election: JD Vance's Missteps," Le Monde.fr, August 1, 2024, https://www.lemonde.fr/en/international/article/2024/08/01/us-presidential-election-jd-vance-s-missteps_6707079_4.html.

As a high-profile political figure, Vance's authenticity has occasionally come under scrutiny. Critics have questioned whether his transition from author to politician has diluted the sincerity that made *Hillbilly Elegy* resonate with so many. Detractors argue that his polished public persona sometimes feels at odds with the raw, vulnerable tone of his memoir. Vance, however, sees this evolution as a natural part of growing into his role as a leader.

Vance's use of social media has, at times, come under fire for his provocative statements. Using tactics inspired by Trump, he has engaged in online feuds and is known for his blunt and inflammatory posts, polarizing readers. Some colleagues view his social media posting style as a break with traditional political communication norms.

Even Vance's offhand comments and appearance have drawn controversy. Trending search topics in 2024 included "JD Vance couch" and "JD Vance eyeliner."

Finally, Vance has championed ideas that some consider controversial. These include his suggestion that the federal government allowed fentanyl into the U.S. to harm conservative voters and alleging that Haitian immigrants were abducting pets in Ohio. He has also praised Alex Jones, considered by some to be a conspiracy theorist, and supported Donald Trump's conviction that the 2020 election was stolen.

The media's portrayal of Vance has been mixed. While some outlets highlight his compelling life story and political acumen, others focus on perceived inconsistencies or controversial remarks. Vance's response has been to embrace the criticism, framing it as a sign of his relevance in the national conversation.

For Vance, controversy has been both a challenge and an opportunity for growth. Each critique, whether fair or unfounded, has prompted reflection and, at times, recalibration.

Navigating public life has required Vance to develop a thick skin while remaining open to constructive feedback. His ability to stay focused on his goals, even in the face of intense scrutiny, speaks to his resilience and commitment to service.

Controversy and criticism have been defining elements of Vance's journey, shaping his leadership style and strengthening his resolve. While detractors question his motives or methods, Vance continues to focus on the issues that matter most to him: empowering working-class Americans, addressing systemic challenges, and restoring faith in the American Dream.

Such situations are inevitable for figures in the public eye, and Vance has dealt with these situations with integrity and grace. In the end, Vance's legacy will be defined not by the controversies he faced but by how he responded to them—with resilience, humility, and complete commitment to his values.

"We must dare to be great; and we must realize that greatness is the fruit of toil and sacrifice and high courage." — Theodore Roosevelt

Vice Presidency and Beyond

JD Vance's rise from a troubled childhood in Middletown, Ohio, to the highest echelons of American politics is a testament to resilience, ambition, and a deep-seated desire to serve. His journey, chronicled in the pages of *Hillbilly Elegy* and lived out on the national stage, has been defined by a willingness to confront adversity and embrace hard truths. From the steel mills and struggling households of Appalachia to the halls of Yale Law School and the U.S. Capitol, Vance's life story is a vivid portrait of the American Dream—hard-earned and never taken for granted.

Throughout his career, Vance has drawn from his personal experiences to advocate for the forgotten, championing the struggles of working-class families and rural communities. His story resonates not just because of its extraordinary trajectory but because of the relatable values it embodies: hard work, perseverance, and an unshakable belief in the power of opportunity.

Vance's path has been a series of significant achievements, each a reflection of his dedication and focus. His memoir, *Hillbilly Elegy*, brought the struggles of Appalachia into the national conversation, sparking debates and shining a light on issues often ignored. His Senate career demonstrated his ability to translate his personal convictions into meaningful legislative action, addressing critical challenges like the opioid epidemic and economic revitalization.

Now, as vice president, Vance stands at the pinnacle of his public service career, representing not only the people of Ohio but also the millions of Americans who see in him a voice for their own aspirations and frustrations. Along the way, he has faced his share of controversies and criticism, yet these challenges have only sharpened his resolve and strengthened his leadership.

As Vance looks to the future, he stands poised to leave an indelible mark on the nation. His vice presidency represents an opportunity not just to influence policy but to reshape the narrative around leadership in America. By staying true to his values and addressing the pressing concerns of working-class families, Vance has the potential to bridge divides and create lasting change.

Whether through initiatives aimed at economic growth, education reform, or tackling the opioid crisis, Vance's priorities remain grounded in the needs of those who feel left behind. His role in the nation's second-highest office offers a platform to amplify these issues and push for solutions that reflect his belief in the promise of the American Dream.

While Vance's story is still being written, certain themes are already clear. His legacy will be defined by his ability to overcome adversity, his dedication to the people he serves, and his unwavering commitment to creating opportunities for those who need them most. As he continues to navigate the complexities of public life, Vance's focus on resilience and advocacy will guide him, ensuring that his leadership is both purposeful and impactful.

Vance's journey has been one of transformation—not just for himself but for the communities and causes he represents. From Middletown to the national stage, he has shown that leadership is about more than titles or achievements; it's about staying true to your roots, learning from criticism, and striving to make a difference.

As Vance steps further into his role as vice president, the road ahead will undoubtedly bring new challenges and opportunities. Yet, if his journey thus far is any indication, he will continue to lead with the same determination and conviction that have defined his life. For Vance, the future offers a chance most Americans only dream of: the chance to help mold the story of America itself.

*　　*　　*

JD Vance has a vision for America, and it is deeply shaped by his own millennial upbringing in a struggling working-class family. He has long emphasized that the challenges he witnessed firsthand— addiction, poverty, and economic despair—are not unique to Appalachia but resonate across rural and industrial communities nationwide. This perspective has fueled his unwavering commitment to advocating for policies that address the needs of working-class Americans, whom he believes have been left behind by decades of economic and political neglect.

Central to Vance's vision is revitalizing struggling communities through targeted economic development. As vice president, he has championed policies to rebuild manufacturing in the heartland, create incentives for businesses to invest in rural areas, and prioritize infrastructure improvements. These initiatives, he argues, are not just about creating jobs but about restoring dignity and opportunity to regions that feel forgotten.

Vance's vision also emphasizes the importance of education reform and healthcare initiatives in lifting up working-class families. He has called for strengthening vocational training and apprenticeships as viable alternatives to four-year college degrees, ensuring that young people in rural and underserved areas have access to pathways that lead to stable, well-paying jobs.

In healthcare, Vance has prioritized expanding access to treatment for addiction and mental health services, particularly in regions hardest hit by the opioid crisis. His initiatives include increasing funding for rural recovery centers and holding pharmaceutical companies accountable for their role in the epidemic.

In an era of deep political polarization, Vance envisions a future where America's cultural and economic divides can be bridged through empathy and shared purpose. Drawing from his experiences as someone who has navigated both the working-class struggles of his youth and the elite corridors of Yale and Washington, Vance believes he is uniquely positioned to foster understanding between disparate groups.

His speeches often focus on the idea that the struggles of working-class families, whether in rural Ohio or urban centers, are more similar than they are different. By framing issues like education, healthcare, and economic opportunity as common ground, Vance has sought to engage both sides of the political spectrum in meaningful dialogue.

Vance's efforts to bridge divides extend to his approach to policymaking. As a Senator and now vice president, he has worked to find common ground with lawmakers from both parties on issues like rural broadband expansion, workforce development, and combating addiction. While his conservative principles remain clear, Vance has demonstrated a willingness to listen and collaborate, earning respect even from some of his critics.

Vance's vision for America is as ambitious as it is personal. It reflects his belief that every American, regardless of where they come from, deserves a chance to thrive. By addressing the struggles of the working class, fostering unity, and bridging divides, JD hopes to not only restore faith in the American Dream but also create a country where opportunity is truly within reach for all.

*   *   *

As vice president, JD Vance has already begun to make his mark on key national issues, but his role in shaping the future of the Republican Party and the nation remains a work in progress. From his efforts to address the opioid crisis and revitalize American manufacturing to his advocacy for rural development and education reform, Vance has established himself as a voice for the forgotten communities of America. His policy priorities reflect a broader vision of bridging economic and cultural divides while creating opportunities for those who feel left behind.

For cxamplc, in his first major international speech as vice president at the AI Action Summit in Paris on February 10 and 11, 2025, Vance led the U.S. initiative to refrain from signing the declaration on "inclusive" artificial intelligence. Framing it as "AI opportunity," he indicated his belief that we are about to enter a second industrial revolution that has "countless revolutionary applications in economic innovation, job creation, national security, health care, free expression and beyond." His stance on regulation could not have been more clear: "To restrict its development now," he said, "will not only unfairly benefit incumbents in this space, it would mean paralysing one of the most promising technologies we have seen in generations."[9]

Days later, he stunned audiences at the Munich Security Conference with his pointed critiques of Europe and what he described as its retreat from its "most fundamental values,"[10] questioning the long-held alliance between Europe and the United States. Expressing doubts about the existence of a shared agenda, his remarks shocked European politicians and earned praise from unexpected audiences, including a Russian TV correspondent who described it gleefully as a "public caning." While the full impact of the ominous warning Vance delivered is yet to become clear, it's certain that he is at the center of what is likely to become a fundamental shift in the international order.

Closer to home, observers see Vance as uniquely positioned to influence the Republican Party's trajectory, particularly as it seeks to balance traditional conservative principles with the populist wave that has redefined its base. His ability to connect with both rural and suburban voters has made him a key figure in fostering unity within the party and appealing to a broader electorate.

---

[9] Reuters, "Quotes from US Vice President JD Vance's AI Speech in Paris," Reuters, February 11, 2025, https://www.reuters.com/technology/quotes-us-vice-president-jd-vances-ai-speech-paris-2025-02-11/.

[10] "JD Vance Stuns Munich Conference with Blistering Attack on Europe's Leaders," The Guardian, February 14, 2025, https://www.theguardian.com/us-news/2025/feb/14/jd-vance-stuns-munich-conference-with-blistering-attack-on-europes-leaders.

With his rapid ascent from author to Senator to vice president, speculation about JD Vance's future ambitions is inevitable. Political commentators have frequently suggested that his vice presidency could serve as a stepping stone toward a presidential bid. Vance himself has remained noncommittal on the topic, focusing instead on his current responsibilities.

Nonetheless, Vance's leadership style, personal narrative, and policy focus position him as a potential contender for higher office. Should he decide to pursue the presidency, his ability to unite factions within the Republican Party and articulate a compelling vision for the nation could make him a formidable candidate.

As Vance looks to the years ahead, the challenges he faces are significant, but so are the opportunities to make a lasting impact. From addressing economic inequality and healthcare disparities to fostering bipartisan collaboration, Vance's leadership will be tested on multiple fronts. Yet, his resilience, dedication, and commitment to service position him to navigate these challenges with integrity and purpose.

For Vance, the journey is about leaving a legacy of meaningful change—one that reflects the values of family, community, and opportunity. As he continues to balance the demands of public service with his personal life, Vance's leadership will be a testament to the enduring potential of perseverance and vision in shaping a better future for America.

JD Vance's story, from the struggling streets of Middletown to the halls of power in Washington, is a testament to the enduring strength of hope. His journey exemplifies the belief that no matter how dire one's circumstances may seem, resilience, determination, and opportunity can pave the way to a better future. As vice president, Vance carries this message of hope to the millions of Americans who feel left behind by economic shifts, political inaction, and cultural divides.

From his story, we can plainly see that resilience, hope, and opportunity has the power to transform not only individual lives but also the trajectory of a nation. Vance's belief in the American dream is a call to action for others to pursue their own potential and work toward a better future.

All else aside, Vice President JD Vance's vision for America remains grounded in the values of perseverance, empathy, and service that have defined his life thus far. The work is far from over—but with hope as his guiding principle, the possibilities for unity and progress are limitless.

Bibliography

Chernova, Yuliya. "Venture firm Narya sees boost in interest after co ..." WSJ. https://www.wsj.com/articles/venture-firm-narya-sees-boost-in-interest-after-co-founder-jd-vances-nomination-6db1debd.

Fowler, Stephen. "JD Vance Vows to Fight for 'forgotten Communities' in Hometown Rally." NPR, July 22, 2024. https://www.npr.org/2024/07/22/nx-s1-5048679/jd-vance-middletown-ohio-rally-kamala-harris-joe-biden.

"Hell of a Speech': JD Vance Commends Donald Trump's Inaugural Address." YouTube, January 20, 2025. https://www.youtube.com/watch?v=LvjUmTsAIMc.

"Hillbilly elegy" author J.D. Vance starts Venture Capital Fund in Ohio. Accessed February 15, 2025. https://www.axios.com/2020/01/09/jd-vance-venture-capital-fund-ohio-silicon-valley-peter-thiel.

"JD Vance." Wikipedia. https://en.wikipedia.org/wiki/JD_Vance

"JD Vance Stuns Munich Conference with Blistering Attack on Europe's Leaders." The Guardian, February 14, 2025. https://www.theguardian.com/us-news/2025/feb/14/jd-vance-stuns-munich-conference-with-blistering-attack-on-europes-leaders.

"JD Vance Tells Republican Convention 'people Who Govern This Country Have Failed and Failed Again' – as It Happened." The Guardian, July 18, 2024. https://www.theguardian.com/us-news/live/2024/jul/17/rnc-jd-vance-speech-trump-day-3-live-updates.

Main, Alison, and Eric Bradner. "Trump Selected Ohio Sen. JD Vance, a Critic Turned Ally, as Running Mate after Last-Minute Push from Son | CNN Politics." CNN, July 16, 2024. https://edition.cnn.com/2024/07/15/politics/trump-vp-pick-jd-vance/index.html.

"Addressing America's Most Acute Problems." NARYA.
	https://naryavc.com/.

Paris, Gilles. "US Presidential Election: JD Vance's Missteps." Le Monde.fr,
	August 1, 2024.
	https://www.lemonde.fr/en/international/article/2024/08/01/us-
	presidential-election-jd-vance-s-missteps_6707079_4.html.

Reuters. "Quotes from US Vice President JD Vance's AI Speech in Paris."
	Reuters, February 11, 2025.
	https://www.reuters.com/technology/quotes-us-vice-president-jd-
	vances-ai-speech-paris-2025-02-11/.

Samuel, Sigal. "JD Vance Accidentally Directed Us to a Crucial Moral
	Question." Vox, February 6, 2025. https://www.vox.com/future-
	perfect/398460/jd-vance-ordo-amoris-order-love-christianity-catholic-
	charity.

Shafiq, Shaman. "Video Shows JD Vance Take Oath as 50th Vice President
	on Inauguration Day." USA Today, n.d.
	https://eu.usatoday.com/story/news/politics/2025/01/20/jd-vance-
	oath-vice-president-video/77840557007/.

Smith, Peter. "A Short Honeymoon for Catholics in D.C. as Vice President
	Vance Clashes with Bishops on Migration." AP News, February 6,
	2025. https://apnews.com/article/jd-vance-catholic-bishops-
	migration-94138954824b68dbd0b29b28504e056e.

Team, Revolution. "Revolution Statement on Vice Presidential Candidate JD
	Vance." Medium, July 25, 2024.
	https://blog.revolution.com/revolution-statement-on-vice-presidential-
	candidate-jd-vance-c1fedf2494d5.

Vance, J. D. *Hillbilly Elegy*. New York, NY: HarperCollins Books, 2016.

Wysong, David. "A Look at Where Usha Vance Got Her Outfits from and
	Their Approximate Prices." The Enquirer, January 21, 2025.

https://eu.cincinnati.com/story/news/politics/2025/01/20/usha-vance-fashion-where-inauguration-outfits-from/77835934007/.

Thank You for Purchasing This Book!

I greatly appreciate you taking the time to read it, and I hope you enjoyed it.

If you have a moment, please consider leaving a review on the platform on which you purchased it. Letting other readers know your thoughts is the most valuable thing you can do for authors and independent researchers like me.

With deep gratitude,

Preston D. Munro

Made in the USA
Columbia, SC
25 April 2025

57149372R00105